MznLnx

Missing Links Exam Preps

Exam Prep for

Managerial Economics in a Global Economy

Salvatore, 5th Edition

The MznLnx Exam Prep is your link from the texbook and lecture to your exams.
The MznLnx Exam Preps are unauthorized and comprehensive reviews of your textbooks.

All material provided by MznLnx and Rico Publications (c) 2010
Textbook publishers and textbook authors do not particpate in or contribute to these reviews.

MznLnx

Rico Publications

Exam Prep for Managerial Economics in a Global Economy
5th Edition
Salvatore

Publisher: Raymond Houge
Assistant Editor: Michael Rouger
Text and Cover Designer: Lisa Buckner
Marketing Manager: Sara Swagger
Project Manager, Editorial Production: Jerry Emerson
Art Director: Vernon Lowerui

Product Manager: Dave Mason
Editorial Assitant: Rachel Guzmanji
Pedagogy: Debra Long
Cover Image: Jim Reed/Getty Images
Text and Cover Printer: City Printing, Inc.
Compositor: Media Mix, Inc.

(c) 2010 Rico Publications
ALL RIGHTS RESERVED. No part of this work covered by the copyright may be reproduced or used in any form or by an means--graphic, electronic, or mechanical, including photocopying, recording, taping, Web distribution, information storage, and retrieval systems, or in any other manner--without the written permission of the publisher.

For more information about our products, contact us at:
Dave.Mason@RicoPublications.com

For permission to use material from this text or product, submit a request online to:
Dave.Mason@RicoPublications.com

Printed in the United States
ISBN:

Contents

CHAPTER 1
The Nature and Scope of Managerial Economics — 1

CHAPTER 2
Optimization Techniques and New Management Tools — 12

CHAPTER 3
Demand Theory — 20

CHAPTER 4
Demand Estimation — 26

CHAPTER 5
Demand Forecasting — 32

CHAPTER 6
Production Theory and Estimation — 38

CHAPTER 7
Cost Theory and Estimation — 44

CHAPTER 8
Market Structure: Perfect Competition, Monopoly, and Monopolistic Competition — 51

CHAPTER 9
Oligopoly and Firm Architecture — 58

CHAPTER 10
Game Theory and Strategic Behavior — 66

CHAPTER 11
Pricing Practices — 69

CHAPTER 12
Regulation and Antitrust: The Role of Government in the Economy — 75

CHAPTER 13
Risk Analysis — 88

CHAPTER 14
Long-Run Investment Decisions: Capital Budgeting — 97

ANSWER KEY — 107

TO THE STUDENT

COMPREHENSIVE

The *MznLnx* Exam Prep series is designed to help you pass your exams. Editors at MznLnx review your textbooks and then prepare these practice exams to help you master the textbook material. Unlike study guides, workbooks, and practice tests provided by the texbook publisher and textbook authors, *MznLnx* gives you **all** of the material in each chapter in exam form, not just samples, so you can be sure to nail your exam.

MECHANICAL

The MznLnx Exam Prep series creates exams that will help you learn the subject matter as well as test you on your understanding. Each question is designed to help you master the concept. Just working through the exams, you gain an understanding of the subject--its a simple mechanical process that produces success.

INTEGRATED STUDY GUIDE AND REVIEW

MznLnx is not just a set of exams designed to test you, its also a comprehensive review of the subject content. Each exam question is also a review of the concept, making sure that you will get the answer correct without having to go to other sources of material. You learn as you go! Its the easiest way to pass an exam.

HUMOR

Studying can be tedious and dry. MznLnx's instructional design includes moderate humor within the exam questions on occassion, to break the tedium and revitalize the brain

Chapter 1. The Nature and Scope of Managerial Economics 1

1. A _____ is:

   - Rewrite _____, in generative grammar and computer science
   - Standardization, a formal and widely-accepted statement, fact, definition, or qualification
   - Operation, a determinate _____ for performing a mathematical operation and obtaining a certain result (Mathematics, Logic)
     - Unary operation
     - Binary operation
   - _____ of inference, a function from sets of formulae to formulae (Mathematics, Logic)
   - _____ of thumb, principle with broad application that is not intended to be strictly accurate or reliable for every situation. Also often simply referred to as a _____
   - Moral, an atomic element of a moral code for guiding choices in human behavior
   - Heuristic, a quantized '_____' which shows a tendency or probability for successful function
   - A regulation, as in sports
   - A Production _____, as in computer science
   - Procedural law, a _____ set governing the application of laws to cases
     - A law, which may informally be called a '_____'
     - A court ruling, a decision by a court
   - In the U.S. Government, a regulation mandated by Congress, but written or expanded upon by the Executive Branch.
   - Norm (sociology), an informal but widely accepted _____, concept, truth, definition, or qualification (social norms, legal norms, coding norms)
   - Norm (philosophy), a kind of sentence or a reason to act, feel or believe
   - 'Rulership' is the concept of governance by a government:
     - Military _____, governance by a military body
     - Monastic _____, a collection of precepts that guides the life of monks or nuns in a religious order where the superior holds the place of Christ
   - Slide _____

   - '_____,' a song by Ayumi Hamasaki
   - '_____,' a song by rapper Nas
   - '_____s,' an album by the band The Whitest Boy Alive
   - _____s: Pyaar Ka Superhit Formula, a 2003 Bollywood film
   - ruler, an instrument for measuring lengths
   - _____, a component of an astrolabe, circumferator or similar instrument
   - The _____s, a bestselling self-help book
   - _____ Project (Run Up-to-date Linux Everywhere), a project that aims to use up-to-date Linux software on old PCs
   - _____ engine, a software system that helps managing business _____s
   - Ja _____, a hip hop artist
     - R.U.L.E., a 2005 greatest hits album by rapper Ja _____
   - '_____s,' a KMFDM song

   a. Rule
   c. Technocracy
   b. Demand
   d. Procter ' Gamble

Chapter 1. The Nature and Scope of Managerial Economics

2. _____, is a branch of economics that applies microeconomic analysis to decision methods of businesses or other management units. As such, it bridges economic theory and economics in practice. It draws heavily from quantitative techniques such as regression analysis and correlation, Lagrangian calculus (linear.)

   a. Forward exchange market
   b. Club goods
   c. Black-Litterman model
   d. Managerial economics

3. _____s is the social science that studies the production, distribution, and consumption of goods and services. The term _____s comes from the Ancient Greek oá¼°κονομῖα from oá¼¶κος (oikos, 'house') + vÏŒμος (nomos, 'custom' or 'law'), hence 'rules of the house(hold)'. Current _____ models developed out of the broader field of political economy in the late 19th century, owing to a desire to use an empirical approach more akin to the physical sciences.

   a. Opportunity cost
   b. Inflation
   c. Energy economics
   d. Economic

4. _____s is concerned with the tasks of developing and applying quantitative or statistical methods to the study and elucidation of economic principles. _____s combines economic theory with statistics to analyze and test economic relationships. Theoretical _____s considers questions about the statistical properties of estimators and tests, while applied _____s is concerned with the application of _____ methods to assess economic theories.

   a. Econometric
   b. Economic
   c. Experimental economics
   d. Evolutionary economics

5. _____ is a branch of economics that deals with the performance, structure, and behavior of a national or regional economy as a whole. Along with microeconomics, _____ is one of the two most general fields in economics. It is the study of the behavior and decision-making of entire economies.

   a. Tobit model
   b. Nominal value
   c. Macroeconomics
   d. New Trade Theory

6. _____ refers to the application of mathematical methods to represent economic theories and analyze problems posed in economics. It allows formulation and derivation of key relationships in a theory with clarity, generality, rigor, and simplicity. Mathematics allows economists to form meaningful, testable propositions about wide-ranging and complex subjects which could not be adequately expressed informally.

   a. Mathematical economics
   b. General equilibrium
   c. Keynesian theory
   d. Rational choice theory

7. _____ is a branch of economics that studies how individuals, households and firms and some states make decisions to allocate limited resources, typically in markets where goods or services are being bought and sold. _____ examines how these decisions and behaviours affect the supply and demand for goods and services, which determines prices; and how prices, in turn, determine the supply and demand of goods and services.

Whereas macroeconomics involves the 'sum total of economic activity, dealing with the issues of growth, inflation and unemployment, and with national economic policies relating to these issues' and the effects of government actions on them.

   a. Countercyclical
   b. New Keynesian economics
   c. Microeconomics
   d. Recession

Chapter 1. The Nature and Scope of Managerial Economics

8. _____ is one of the four Ps of the marketing mix. The other three aspects are product, promotion, and place. It is also a key variable in microeconomic price allocation theory.

   a. Point of total assumption
   b. Guaranteed Maximum Price
   c. Premium pricing
   d. Pricing

9. _____ is a way of expressing knowledge or belief that an event will occur or has occurred. In mathematics the concept has been given an exact meaning in _____ theory, that is used extensively in such areas of study as mathematics, statistics, finance, gambling, science, and philosophy to draw conclusions about the likelihood of potential events and the underlying mechanics of complex systems.

   The word _____ does not have a consistent direct definition.

   a. 100-year flood
   b. 130-30 fund
   c. Probability
   d. 1921 recession

10. In probability theory and statistics, a _____ identifies either the probability of each value of an unidentified random variable (when the variable is discrete), or the probability of the value falling within a particular interval (when the variable is continuous.) The _____ describes the range of possible values that a random variable can attain and the probability that the value of the random variable is within any (measurable) subset of that range. The Normal distribution, often called the 'bell curve'

   When the random variable takes values in the set of real numbers, the _____ is completely described by the cumulative distribution function, whose value at each real x is the probability that the random variable is smaller than or equal to x.

   a. 100-year flood
   b. Probability distribution
   c. 1921 recession
   d. 130-30 fund

11. In mathematics, a _____ is a constant multiplicative factor of a certain object. For example, in the expression $9x^2$, the _____ of x^2 is 9.

   The object can be such things as a variable, a vector, a function, etc.

   a. 100-year flood
   b. 1921 recession
   c. 130-30 fund
   d. Coefficient

12. _____ in its literal sense is the process of transformation of local or regional phenomena into global ones. It can be described as a process by which the people of the world are unified into a single society and function together.

   This process is a combination of economic, technological, sociocultural and political forces.

   a. Helsinki Process on Globalisation and Democracy
   b. Globalization
   c. Global Cosmopolitanism
   d. Globally Integrated Enterprise

13. In economics and related disciplines, a _____ is a cost incurred in making an economic exchange. For example, most people, when buying or selling a stock, must pay a commission to their broker; that commission is a _____ of doing the stock deal. Or consider buying a banana from a store; to purchase the banana, your costs will be not only the price of the banana itself, but also the energy and effort it requires to find out which of the various banana products you prefer, where to get them and at what price, the cost of traveling from your house to the store and back, the time waiting in line, and the effort of the paying itself; the costs above and beyond the cost of the banana are the _____s.

a. Sliding scale fees
b. Cost of poor quality
c. Cost allocation
d. Transaction cost

14. In economics, the term _____ of income or _____ refers to a simple economic model which describes the reciprocal circulation of income between producers and consumers. In the _____ model, the inter-dependent entities of producer and consumer are referred to as 'firms' and 'households' respectively and provide each other with factors in order to facilitate the flow of income. Firms provide consumers with goods and services in exchange for consumer expenditure and 'factors of production' from households.

a. 130-30 fund
b. 1921 recession
c. 100-year flood
d. Circular flow

15. The _____ consists of a number of economic theories which describe the nature of the firm, company including its existence, its behaviour, and its relationship with the market.

In simplified terms, the _____ aims to answer these questions:

1. Existence - why do firms emerge, why are not all transactions in the economy mediated over the market?
2. Boundaries - why the boundary between firms and the market is located exactly there? Which transactions are performed internally and which are negotiated on the market?
3. Organization - why are firms structured in such specific way? What is the interplay of formal and informal relationships?

Despite looking simple, these questions are not answered by the established economic theory, which usually views firms as given, and treats them as black boxes without any internal structure.

The First World War period saw a change of emphasis in economic theory away from industry-level analysis which mainly included analysing markets to analysis at the level of the firm, as it became increasingly clear that perfect competition was no longer an adequate model of how firms behaved. Economic theory till then had focussed on trying to understand markets alone and there had been little study on understanding why firms or organisations exist.

a. Technology gap
b. Khazzoom-Brookes postulate
c. Policy Ineffectiveness Proposition
d. Theory of the firm

16. _____ is the a method of technical and economic research of the systems for purpose to optimize a parity between system's consumer functions or properties and expenses to achieve those functions or properties.

This methodology for continuous perfection of production, industrial technologies, organizational structures was developed by Juryj Sobolev in 1948 at the 'Perm telephone factory'

- 1948 Juryj Sobolev - the first success in application of a method analysis at the 'Perm telephone factory' .
- 1949 - the first application for the invention as result of use of the new method.

Today in economically developed countries practically each enterprise or the company use methodology of the kind of functional-cost analysis as a practice of the quality management, most full satisfying to principles of standards of series ISO 9000.

- Interest of consumer not in products itself, but the advantage which it will receive from its usage.
- The consumer aspires to reduce his expenses
- Functions needed by consumer can be executed in the various ways, and, hence, with various efficiency and expenses. Among possible alternatives of realization of functions exist such in which the parity of quality and the price is the optimal for the consumer.

The goal of _____ is achievement of the highest consumer satisfaction of production at simultaneous decrease in all kinds of industrial expenses Classical _____ has three English synonyms - Value Engineering, Value Management, Value Analysis.

a. Monopoly wage
c. Staple financing
b. Willingness to pay
d. Function cost analysis

17. Economics:

- _____, the desire to own something and the ability to pay for it
- _____ curve, a graphic representation of a _____ schedule
- _____ deposit, the money in checking accounts
- _____ pull theory, the theory that inflation occurs when _____ for goods and services exceeds existing supplies
- _____ schedule, a table that lists the quantity of a good a person will buy it each different price
- _____ side economics, the school of economics at believes government spending and tax cuts open economy by raising _____

a. Variability
c. McKesson ' Robbins scandal
b. Production
d. Demand

18. _____ is the activity of estimating the quantity of a product or service that consumers will purchase. _____ involves techniques including both informal methods, such as educated guesses, and quantitative methods, such as the use of historical sales data or current data from test markets. _____ may be used in making pricing decisions, in assessing future capacity requirements, or in making decisions on whether to enter a new market.

a. Demand forecasting
b. Financial Reporting
c. Cost price
d. Finance designations

19. In political science and economics, the _____ or agency dilemma treats the difficulties that arise under conditions of incomplete and asymmetric information when a principal hires an agent, such as the problem that the two may not have the same interests, while the principal is, presumably, hiring the agent to pursue the interests of the former.

Various mechanisms may be used to try to align the interests of the agent with those of the principal, such as piece rates/commissions, profit sharing, efficiency wages, performance measurement (including financial statements), the agent posting a bond, or fear of firing. The _____ is found in most employer/employee relationships, for example, when stockholders hire top executives of corporations.

a. Principal-agent problem
b. 1921 recession
c. 130-30 fund
d. 100-year flood

20. _____ is the process of estimation in unknown situations. Prediction is a similar, but more general term. Both can refer to estimation of time series, cross-sectional or longitudinal data.
a. 100-year flood
b. 130-30 fund
c. 1921 recession
d. Forecasting

21. In economics, _____ is the difference between a company's total revenue and its opportunity costs. It is the increase in wealth that an investor has from making an investment, taking into consideration all costs associated with that investment including the opportunity cost of capital.

Profit is the factor income of the entrepreneur.

a. Economic profit
b. Accounting profit
c. ACCRA Cost of Living Index
d. Operating profit

22. An _____ is an easy accounted cost, such as wage, rent and materials. It can be transacted in the form of money payment and is lost directly, as opposed to monetary implicit costs.
a. Explicit cost
b. Average variable cost
c. Inventory valuation
d. Average fixed cost

23. In economics, an _____ occurs when one foregoes an alternative action but does not make an actual payment. (For instance, the explicit cost of a night at the movies includes the moviegoer's ticket and soda, but the _____ includes the pay he would have earned if he had chosen to work instead.) _____s are related to forgone benefits of any single transaction.
a. Implicit cost
b. External sector
c. Ostrich strategy
d. Overnight trade

24. In economics, a _____ exists when a specific individual or enterprise has sufficient control over a particular product or service to determine significantly the terms on which other individuals shall have access to it. Monopolies are thus characterized by a lack of economic competition for the good or service that they provide and a lack of viable substitute goods. The verb 'monopolize' refers to the process by which a firm gains persistently greater market share than what is expected under perfect competition.

a. 1921 recession
c. 100-year flood
b. 130-30 fund
d. Monopoly

25. _____ is the removal or simplification of government rules and regulations that constrain the operation of market forces. _____ does not mean elimination of laws against fraud, but eliminating or reducing government control of how business is done, thereby moving toward a more free market.

The stated rationale for '_____' is often that fewer and simpler regulations will lead to a raised level of competitiveness, therefore higher productivity, more efficiency and lower prices overall.

a. Macroeconomic policy instruments
c. Secular basis
b. Fundamental psychological law
d. Deregulation

26. In economic models, the _____ time frame assumes no fixed factors of production. Firms can enter or leave the marketplace, and the cost (and availability) of land, labor, raw materials, and capital goods can be assumed to vary. In contrast, in the short-run time frame, certain factors are assumed to be fixed, because there is not sufficient time for them to change.

a. Diseconomies of scale
c. Price/performance ratio
b. Productivity world
d. Long-run

27. _____ are made by investors and investment managers.

Investors commonly perform investment analysis by making use of fundamental analysis, technical analysis and gut feel.

_____ are often supported by decision tools.

a. Arbitrage betting
c. Investment decisions
b. Inventory investment
d. Investment strategy

28. _____ is a policy or ideology of violence intended to intimidate or cause terror for the purpose of 'exerting pressure on decision making by state bodies.' The term 'terror' is largely used to indicate clandestine, low-intensity violence that targets civilians and generates public fear. Thus 'terror' is distinct from asymmetric warfare, and violates the concept of a common law of war in which civilian life is regarded. The term '-ism' is used to indicate an ideology --typically one that claims its attacks are in the domain of a 'just war' concept, though most condemn such as crimes against humanity.

a. Terrorism
c. 1921 recession
b. 130-30 fund
d. 100-year flood

Chapter 1. The Nature and Scope of Managerial Economics

29. _____ is a branch of economics with three main subdisciplines international trade, monetary economics and international finance.

- International trade studies goods-and-services flows across international boundaries from supply-and-demand factors, economic integration, and policy variables such as tariff rates and trade quotas.
- International finance studies the flow of capital across international financial markets, and the effects of these movements on exchange rates.
- International monetary economics and macroeconomics studies money and macro flows across countries.
- Stanley W. Black (2008.) 'international monetary institutions,' The New Palgrave Dictionary of Economics. 2nd Edition.

a. Index number
b. Economic depreciation
c. ACCRA Cost of Living Index
d. International economics

30. The _____, a unit of the United States Department of Labor, is the principal fact-finding agency for the U.S. government in the broad field of labor economics and statistics. The BLS is an independent national statistical agency that collects, processes, analyzes, and disseminates essential statistical data to the American public, the U.S. Congress, other Federal agencies, State and local governments, business, and labor representatives. The BLS also serves as a statistical resource to the Department of Labor.

a. Gross world product
b. Bureau of Labor Statistics
c. Gross national product
d. Gross Regional Product

31. A _____ is the procedure of systematically acquiring and recording information about the members of a given population. It is a regularly occurring and official count of a particular population. The term is used mostly in connection with national 'population and door to door _____es' (to be taken every 10 years according to United Nations recommendations), agriculture, and business _____es.

a. 100-year flood
b. Census
c. 1921 recession
d. 130-30 fund

32. An _____ is a statistic about the economy. _____s allow analysis of economic performance and predictions of future performance.

_____s include various indices, earnings reports, and economic summaries, such as unemployment, housing starts, Consumer Price Index (a measure for inflation), industrial production, bankruptcies, Gross Domestic Product, broadband internet penetration, retail sales, stock market prices, and money supply changes.

a. ACCRA Cost of Living Index
b. Economic Vulnerability Index
c. Internationalization Index
d. Economic Indicator

Chapter 1. The Nature and Scope of Managerial Economics

33. The _____ is the central banking system of the United States. Created in 1913 by the enactment of the Federal Reserve Act (signed by Woodrow Wilson), it is a quasi-public and quasi-private (government entity with private components) banking system that comprises (1) the presidentially appointed Board of Governors of the _____ in Washington, D.C.; (2) the Federal Open Market Committee; (3) twelve regional Federal Reserve Banks located in major cities throughout the nation acting as fiscal agents for the U.S. Treasury, each with its own nine-member board of directors; (4) numerous other private U.S. member banks, which subscribe to required amounts of non-transferable stock in their regional Federal Reserve Banks; and (5) various advisory councils. Since February 2006, Ben Bernanke has served as the Chairman of the Board of Governors of the _____.

   a. Monetary Policy Report to the Congress
   b. Federal Reserve System Open Market Account
   c. Term auction facility
   d. Federal Reserve System

34. The _____ is an international organization that oversees the global financial system by following the macroeconomic policies of its member countries, in particular those with an impact on exchange rates and the balance of payments. It is an organization formed to stabilize international exchange rates and facilitate development. It also offers financial and technical assistance to its members, making it an international lender of last resort.

   a. ACEA agreement
   b. ACCRA Cost of Living Index
   c. Office of Thrift Supervision
   d. International Monetary Fund

35. The _____ is an international financial institution that provides financial and technical assistance to developing countries for development programs (e.g. bridges, roads, schools, etc.) with the stated goal of reducing poverty.

The _____ differs from the _____ Group, in that the _____ comprises only two institutions:

- International Bank for Reconstruction and Development (IBRD)
- International Development Association (IDA)

Whereas the latter incorporates these two in addition to three more:

- International Finance Corporation (IFC)
- Multilateral Investment Guarantee Agency (MIGA)
- International Centre for Settlement of Investment Disputes (ICSID)

John Maynard Keynes (right) represented the UK at the conference, and Harry Dexter White represented the US.

The _____ is one of two major financial institutions created as a result of the Bretton Woods Conference in 1944. The International Monetary Fund, a related but separate institution, is the second.

   a. Flow to Equity-Approach
   b. Financial costs of the 2003 Iraq War
   c. World Bank
   d. Bank-State-Branch

36. The _____ is an important selective, mainly private, international organization designed by its founders to supervise and liberalize international trade. The organization officially commenced on 1 January 1995, under the Marrakesh Agreement, succeeding the 1947 General Agreement on Tariffs and Trade (GATT.)

The _____ deals with regulation of trade between participating countries; it provides a framework for negotiating and formalising trade agreements, and a dispute resolution process aimed at enforcing participants' adherence to _____ agreements which are signed by representatives of member governments and ratified by their parliaments.

   a. 2009 G-20 London summit protests
   b. World Trade Organization
   c. Bio-energy village
   d. Backus-Kehoe-Kydland consumption correlation puzzle

37. _____ is money accepted for exchange of goods in an economy. The prevalence of one money over another arises, usually, when a government designates through decrees that the government shall accept only particular notes and coins in payment for taxes. Typically, money of _____ consists of stamped coins and minted paper bills.
   a. Security thread
   b. Totnes pound
   c. Local currency
   d. Currency

38. In finance, the _____s between two currencies specifies how much one currency is worth in terms of the other. It is the value of a foreign natione;s currency in terms of the home natione;s currency. For example an _____ of 102 Japanese yen to the United States dollar means that JPY 102 is worth the same as USD 1.
   a. Interbank market
   b. ACEA agreement
   c. ACCRA Cost of Living Index
   d. Exchange rate

39. A _____ is a public market for the trading of company stock and derivatives at an agreed price; these are securities listed on a stock exchange as well as those only traded privately.

The size of the world _____ was estimated at about $36.6 trillion US at the beginning of October 2008 . The total world derivatives market has been estimated at about $791 trillion face or nominal value, 11 times the size of the entire world economy.

   a. Stock market
   b. Adam Smith
   c. Adolf Hitler
   d. Adolph Fischer

40. A _____ is a method of measuring a section of the stock market. Many indices are cited by news or financial services firms and are used to benchmark the performance of portfolios such as mutual funds.

Stock market indices may be classed in many ways.

   a. Stock market index
   b. Scrip issue
   c. Lock up period
   d. Stock market bubble

41. In economics, the _____ can be defined as the graph depicting the relationship between the price of a certain commodity, and the amount of it that consumers are willing and able to purchase at that given price. It is a graphic representation of a demand schedule. The _____ for all consumers together follows from the _____ of every individual consumer: the individual demands at each price are added together.

a. Kuznets curve
b. Cost curve
c. Wage curve
d. Demand curve

42. _____ in economics and business is the result of an exchange and from that trade we assign a numerical monetary value to a good, service or asset. If Alice trades Bob 4 apples for an orange, the _____ of an orange is 4 apples. Inversely, the _____ of an apple is 1/4 oranges.
   a. Price book
   b. Price
   c. Premium pricing
   d. Price war

43. _____ is an economic model based on price, utility and quantity in a market. It predicts that in a competitive market, price will function to equalize the quantity demanded by consumers, and the quantity supplied by producers, resulting in an economic equilibrium of price and quantity. The model incorporates other factors changing equilibrium as a shift of demand and/or supply.
   a. Joint demand
   b. Rational addiction
   c. Deferred gratification
   d. Supply and demand

44. In economics, _____ is when quantity demanded is more than quantity supplied. See Economic shortage.
   a. ACEA agreement
   b. ACCRA Cost of Living Index
   c. AD-IA Model
   d. Excess demand

45. In economics, _____ is when quantity supplied is more than quantity demanded. .
   a. Economic Value Creation
   b. Effective unemployment rate
   c. Illicit financial flows
   d. Excess supply

Chapter 2. Optimization Techniques and New Management Tools

1. _____ is one of the four Ps of the marketing mix. The other three aspects are product, promotion, and place. It is also a key variable in microeconomic price allocation theory.
   a. Guaranteed Maximum Price
   b. Premium pricing
   c. Point of total assumption
   d. Pricing

2. _____s is the social science that studies the production, distribution, and consumption of goods and services. The term _____s comes from the Ancient Greek oá¼°κονομῖα from oá¼¶κος (oikos, 'house') + vÏŒμος (nomos, 'custom' or 'law'), hence 'rules of the house(hold)'. Current _____ models developed out of the broader field of political economy in the late 19th century, owing to a desire to use an empirical approach more akin to the physical sciences.
   a. Inflation
   b. Opportunity cost
   c. Energy economics
   d. Economic

3. _____ is the total money received from the sale of any given quantity of output.

The _____ is calculated by taking the price of the sale times the quantity sold, i.e.

_____ = price X quantity.

   a. Small numbers game
   b. Market development funds
   c. Ceteris paribus
   d. Total revenue

4. In economics and finance, _____ is the change in total cost that arises when the quantity produced changes by one unit. It is the cost of producing one more unit of a good. Mathematically, the _____ function is expressed as the first derivative of the total cost (TC) function with respect to quantity (Q.)
   a. Khozraschyot
   b. Variable cost
   c. Quality costs
   d. Marginal cost

5. In economics, and cost accounting, _____ describes the total economic cost of production and is made up of variable costs, which vary according to the quantity of a good produced and include inputs such as labor and raw materials, plus fixed costs, which are independent of the quantity of a good produced and include inputs (capital) that cannot be varied in the short term, such as buildings and machinery. _____ in economics includes the total opportunity cost of each factor of production in addition to fixed and variable costs.

The rate at which _____ changes as the amount produced changes is called marginal cost.

   a. 130-30 fund
   b. Total cost
   c. 100-year flood
   d. 1921 recession

6. In economics, _____ is equal to total cost divided by the number of goods produced (the output quantity, Q.) It is also equal to the sum of average variable costs (total variable costs divided by Q) plus average fixed costs (total fixed costs divided by Q.) _____s may be dependent on the time period considered (increasing production may be expensive or impossible in the short term, for example.)
   a. Average cost
   b. Average fixed cost
   c. Average variable cost
   d. Explicit cost

Chapter 2. Optimization Techniques and New Management Tools

7. In economics, a _____ is a graph of the costs of production as a function of total quantity produced. In a free market economy, productively efficient firms use these curves to find the optimal point of production, where they make the most profits. There are a few different types of _____s, each relevant to a different area of economics.
    a. Kuznets curve
    b. Demand curve
    c. Phillips curve
    d. Cost curve

8. In microeconomics, _____ is the extra revenue that an additional unit of product will bring. It is the additional income from selling one more unit of a good; sometimes equal to price. It can also be described as the change in total revenue/change in number of units sold.
    a. Marginal revenue
    b. Reservation price
    c. Long term
    d. Market demand schedule

9. In economics, _____ is the process by which a firm determines the price and output level that returns the greatest profit. There are several approaches to this problem. The total revenue--total cost method relies on the fact that profit equals revenue minus cost, and the marginal revenue--marginal cost method is based on the fact that total profit in a perfectly competitive market reaches its maximum point where marginal revenue equals marginal cost.
    a. Profit maximization
    b. Normal profit
    c. 100-year flood
    d. Profit margin

10. Competition law, known in the United States as _____ law, has three main elements:

    - prohibiting agreements or practices that restrict free trading and competition between business entities. This includes in particular the repression of cartels.
    - banning abusive behaviour by a firm dominating a market, or anti-competitive practices that tend to lead to such a dominant position. Practices controlled in this way may include predatory pricing, tying, price gouging, refusal to deal, and many others.
    - supervising the mergers and acquisitions of large corporations, including some joint ventures. Transactions that are considered to threaten the competitive process can be prohibited altogether, or approved subject to 'remedies' such as an obligation to divest part of the merged business or to offer licences or access to facilities to enable other businesses to continue competing.

    The substance and practice of competition law varies from jurisdiction to jurisdiction. Protecting the interests of consumers (consumer welfare) and ensuring that entrepreneurs have an opportunity to compete in the market economy are often treated as important objectives. Competition law is closely connected with law on deregulation of access to markets, state aids and subsidies, the privatisation of state owned assets and the establishment of independent sector regulators. In recent decades, competition law has been viewed as a way to provide better public services.

    a. Anti-Inflation Act
    b. United Kingdom competition law
    c. Intellectual property law
    d. Antitrust

Chapter 2. Optimization Techniques and New Management Tools

11. _____, known in the United States as antitrust law, has three main elements:

- prohibiting agreements or practices that restrict free trading and competition between business entities. This includes in particular the repression of cartels.
- banning abusive behaviour by a firm dominating a market, or anti-competitive practices that tend to lead to such a dominant position. Practices controlled in this way may include predatory pricing, tying, price gouging, refusal to deal, and many others.
- supervising the mergers and acquisitions of large corporations, including some joint ventures. Transactions that are considered to threaten the competitive process can be prohibited altogether, or approved subject to 'remedies' such as an obligation to divest part of the merged business or to offer licences or access to facilities to enable other businesses to continue competing.

The substance and practice of _____ varies from jurisdiction to jurisdiction. Protecting the interests of consumers (consumer welfare) and ensuring that entrepreneurs have an opportunity to compete in the market economy are often treated as important objectives. _____ is closely connected with law on deregulation of access to markets, state aids and subsidies, the privatisation of state owned assets and the establishment of independent sector regulators. In recent decades, _____ has been viewed as a way to provide better public services.

a. Competition law
b. Fee simple
c. Due diligence
d. Hostile work environment

12. _____s are financial contracts whose values are derived from the value of something else (known as the underlying.) The underlying value on which a _____ is based can be an asset (e.g., commodities, equities (stocks), residential mortgages, commercial real estate, loans, bonds), an index (e.g., interest rates, exchange rates, stock market indices, consumer price index (CPI) -- see inflation _____s), weather conditions bonds or other forms of credit.

a. 100-year flood
b. Second derivative
c. 130-30 fund
d. Derivative

13. _____ is a common market structure where many competing producers sell products that are differentiated from one another (ie. the products are substitutes, but are not exactly alike.) Many markets are monopolistically competitive, common examples include the markets for restaurants, cereal, clothing, shoes and service industries in large cities.

a. Monopolistic competition
b. Mathematical economics
c. Financial crisis
d. Perfect competition

Chapter 2. Optimization Techniques and New Management Tools

14. A _____ is:

- Rewrite _____, in generative grammar and computer science
- Standardization, a formal and widely-accepted statement, fact, definition, or qualification
- Operation, a determinate _____ for performing a mathematical operation and obtaining a certain result (Mathematics, Logic)
    - Unary operation
    - Binary operation
- _____ of inference, a function from sets of formulae to formulae (Mathematics, Logic)
- _____ of thumb, principle with broad application that is not intended to be strictly accurate or reliable for every situation. Also often simply referred to as a _____
- Moral, an atomic element of a moral code for guiding choices in human behavior
- Heuristic, a quantized '_____' which shows a tendency or probability for successful function
- A regulation, as in sports
- A Production _____, as in computer science
- Procedural law, a _____ set governing the application of laws to cases
    - A law, which may informally be called a '_____'
    - A court ruling, a decision by a court
- In the U.S. Government, a regulation mandated by Congress, but written or expanded upon by the Executive Branch.
- Norm (sociology), an informal but widely accepted _____, concept, truth, definition, or qualification (social norms, legal norms, coding norms)
- Norm (philosophy), a kind of sentence or a reason to act, feel or believe
- 'Rulership' is the concept of governance by a government:
    - Military _____, governance by a military body
    - Monastic _____, a collection of precepts that guides the life of monks or nuns in a religious order where the superior holds the place of Christ
- Slide _____

- '_____,' a song by Ayumi Hamasaki
- '_____,' a song by rapper Nas
- '_____s,' an album by the band The Whitest Boy Alive
- _____s: Pyaar Ka Superhit Formula, a 2003 Bollywood film
- ruler, an instrument for measuring lengths
- _____, a component of an astrolabe, circumferator or similar instrument
- The _____s, a bestselling self-help book
- _____ Project (Run Up-to-date Linux Everywhere), a project that aims to use up-to-date Linux software on old PCs
- _____ engine, a software system that helps managing business _____s
- Ja _____, a hip hop artist
    - R.U.L.E., a 2005 greatest hits album by rapper Ja _____
- '_____s,' a KMFDM song

a. Procter ' Gamble
c. Demand
b. Rule
d. Technocracy

Chapter 2. Optimization Techniques and New Management Tools

15. Economics:

    - _____, the desire to own something and the ability to pay for it
    - _____ curve, a graphic representation of a _____ schedule
    - _____ deposit, the money in checking accounts
    - _____ pull theory, the theory that inflation occurs when _____ for goods and services exceeds existing supplies
    - _____ schedule, a table that lists the quantity of a good a person will buy it each different price
    - _____ side economics, the school of economics at believes government spending and tax cuts open economy by raising _____

    a. Demand
    b. McKesson ' Robbins scandal
    c. Production
    d. Variability

16. _____ is the activity of estimating the quantity of a product or service that consumers will purchase. _____ involves techniques including both informal methods, such as educated guesses, and quantitative methods, such as the use of historical sales data or current data from test markets. _____ may be used in making pricing decisions, in assessing future capacity requirements, or in making decisions on whether to enter a new market.

    a. Cost price
    b. Financial Reporting
    c. Finance designations
    d. Demand forecasting

17. _____ is the process of estimation in unknown situations. Prediction is a similar, but more general term. Both can refer to estimation of time series, cross-sectional or longitudinal data.

    a. 100-year flood
    b. 130-30 fund
    c. 1921 recession
    d. Forecasting

18. Let f be a differentiable function, and let f'(x) be its derivative. The derivative of f'(x) (if it has one) is written f''(x) and is called the _____ of f. Similarly, the derivative of a _____, if it exists, is written f'''(x) and is called the third derivative of f.

    a. 100-year flood
    b. Weighted
    c. 130-30 fund
    d. Second derivative

19. In statistics, _____ refers to techniques for the modeling and analysis of numerical data consisting of values of a dependent variable and of one or more independent variables The dependent variable in the regression equation is modeled as a function of the independent variables, corresponding parameters, and an error term. The error term is treated as a random variable.

    a. 1921 recession
    b. 100-year flood
    c. 130-30 fund
    d. Regression analysis

20. In mathematics, a _____ of a function of several variables is its derivative with respect to one of those variables with the others held constant (as opposed to the total derivative, in which all variables are allowed to vary.) _____s are useful in vector calculus and differential geometry.

    The _____ of a function f with respect to the variable x is written as f'_x, $\partial_x f$, or $\partial f/\partial x$.

a. 130-30 fund
b. 100-year flood
c. 1921 recession
d. Partial derivative

21. A _____ is an object whose consumption increases the utility of the consumer, for which the quantity demanded exceeds the quantity supplied at zero price. _____s are usually modeled as having diminishing marginal utility. The first individual purchase has high utility; the second has less.

a. Merit good
b. Good
c. Pie method
d. Composite good

22. _____ in its literal sense is the process of transformation of local or regional phenomena into global ones. It can be described as a process by which the people of the world are unified into a single society and function together.

This process is a combination of economic, technological, sociocultural and political forces.

a. Globally Integrated Enterprise
b. Helsinki Process on Globalisation and Democracy
c. Globalization
d. Global Cosmopolitanism

23. The _____ consists of a number of economic theories which describe the nature of the firm, company including its existence, its behaviour, and its relationship with the market.

In simplified terms, the _____ aims to answer these questions:

1. Existence - why do firms emerge, why are not all transactions in the economy mediated over the market?
2. Boundaries - why the boundary between firms and the market is located exactly there? Which transactions are performed internally and which are negotiated on the market?
3. Organization - why are firms structured in such specific way? What is the interplay of formal and informal relationships?

Despite looking simple, these questions are not answered by the established economic theory, which usually views firms as given, and treats them as black boxes without any internal structure.

The First World War period saw a change of emphasis in economic theory away from industry-level analysis which mainly included analysing markets to analysis at the level of the firm, as it became increasingly clear that perfect competition was no longer an adequate model of how firms behaved. Economic theory till then had focussed on trying to understand markets alone and there had been little study on understanding why firms or organisations exist.

a. Policy Ineffectiveness Proposition
b. Khazzoom-Brookes postulate
c. Technology gap
d. Theory of the firm

24. The _____ is an important selective, mainly private, international organization designed by its founders to supervise and liberalize international trade. The organization officially commenced on 1 January 1995, under the Marrakesh Agreement, succeeding the 1947 General Agreement on Tariffs and Trade (GATT.)

The _____ deals with regulation of trade between participating countries; it provides a framework for negotiating and formalising trade agreements, and a dispute resolution process aimed at enforcing participants' adherence to _____ agreements which are signed by representatives of member governments and ratified by their parliaments.

a. Backus-Kehoe-Kydland consumption correlation puzzle
b. 2009 G-20 London summit protests
c. Bio-energy village
d. World Trade Organization

25. _____ can be considered to have three main components: quality control, quality assurance and quality improvement. _____ is focused not only on product quality, but also the means to achieve it. _____ therefore uses quality assurance and control of processes as well as products to achieve more consistent quality.

a. 100-year flood
b. Quality management
c. 130-30 fund
d. 1921 recession

26. _____ is a business management strategy, initially implemented by Motorola, that today enjoys widespread application in many sectors of industry.

_____ seeks to improve the quality of process outputs by identifying and removing the causes of defects (errors) and variation in manufacturing and business processes. It uses a set of quality management methods, including statistical methods, and creates a special infrastructure of people within the organization ('Black Belts' etc.)

a. Private sector
b. Tertiary sector of economy
c. Primary sector of the economy
d. Six Sigma

27. _____ AG is an international Universal bank with its headquarters in Frankfurt, Germany. The bank employs more than 81,000 people in 76 countries, and has a large presence in Europe, the Americas, Asia Pacific and the emerging markets.

_____ has offices in major financial centers, such as London, Moscow, New York, São Paulo, Singapore, Sydney, Hong Kong and Tokyo.

a. Chinese correction
b. Paris Club
c. Deutsche Bank
d. Federal Deposit Insurance Corporation

28. _____ relates to decisions that define expectations, grant power, or verify performance. It consists either of a separate process or of a specific part of management or leadership processes. Sometimes people set up a government to administer these processes and systems.

a. 1921 recession
b. 100-year flood
c. Governance
d. 130-30 fund

29. A _____ is a place of residence or refuge and comfort. It is usually a place in which an individual or a family can rest and be able to store personal property. Most modern-day households contain sanitary facilities and a means of preparing food.

a. 1921 recession b. 130-30 fund
c. Home d. 100-year flood

Chapter 3. Demand Theory

1. Economics:

   - _____, the desire to own something and the ability to pay for it
   - _____ curve, a graphic representation of a _____ schedule
   - _____ deposit, the money in checking accounts
   - _____ pull theory, the theory that inflation occurs when _____ for goods and services exceeds existing supplies
   - _____ schedule, a table that lists the quantity of a good a person will buy it each different price
   - _____ side economics, the school of economics at believes government spending and tax cuts open economy by raising _____

   a. Demand
   b. McKesson ' Robbins scandal
   c. Production
   d. Variability

2. A _____ is something for which there is demand, but which is supplied without qualitative differentiation across a market. It is a product that is the same no matter who produces it, such as petroleum, notebook paper, or milk. In other words, copper is copper.

   a. 100-year flood
   b. Hard commodity
   c. Soft commodity
   d. Commodity

3. In consumer theory, an _____ is a good that decreases in demand when consumer income rises, unlike normal goods, for which the opposite is observed. It is a good that consumers demand increases when their income increases. Inferiority, in this sense, is an observable fact relating to affordability rather than a statement about the quality of the good.

   a. Export-oriented
   b. Independent goods
   c. Information good
   d. Inferior good

4. In economics, _____s are any goods for which demand increases when income increases and falls when income decreases but price remains constant, i.e. with a positive income elasticity of demand. The term does not necessarily refer to the quality of the good.

   Depending on the indifference curves, the amount of a good bought can either increase, decrease, or stay the same when income increases.

   a. Financial contagion
   b. Normative economics
   c. Bord halfpenny
   d. Normal good

5. A _____ is an object whose consumption increases the utility of the consumer, for which the quantity demanded exceeds the quantity supplied at zero price. _____s are usually modeled as having diminishing marginal utility. The first individual purchase has high utility; the second has less.

   a. Composite good
   b. Pie method
   c. Merit good
   d. Good

6. In economics, the _____ can be defined as the graph depicting the relationship between the price of a certain commodity, and the amount of it that consumers are willing and able to purchase at that given price. It is a graphic representation of a demand schedule. The _____ for all consumers together follows from the _____ of every individual consumer: the individual demands at each price are added together.

Chapter 3. Demand Theory

a. Kuznets curve
b. Wage curve
c. Cost curve
d. Demand curve

7. In economics, a _____ is a table that lists the quantity of a good a person will buy it each different price See Demand curve.
   a. Federal Reserve districts
   b. Demand schedule
   c. Free contract
   d. Rational irrationality

8. _____ is the observation that people often do and believe things because many other people do and believe the same things. The effect is often pejoratively called herding instinct, particularly when applied to adolescents. People tend to follow the crowd without examining the merits of a particular thing.
   a. Hyperbolic discounting
   b. Bandwagon effect
   c. Halo effect
   d. Sunk costs

9. _____ is the activity of estimating the quantity of a product or service that consumers will purchase. _____ involves techniques including both informal methods, such as educated guesses, and quantitative methods, such as the use of historical sales data or current data from test markets. _____ may be used in making pricing decisions, in assessing future capacity requirements, or in making decisions on whether to enter a new market.
   a. Finance designations
   b. Cost price
   c. Financial Reporting
   d. Demand forecasting

10. The _____ refers to the desire to own exclusive or unique goods. These goods usually have a high economic value, but low practical value. The less of an item available, the higher its snob value.
    a. Cross elasticity of demand
    b. Demand vacuum
    c. Snob effect
    d. Deferred gratification

11. _____ is the process of estimation in unknown situations. Prediction is a similar, but more general term. Both can refer to estimation of time series, cross-sectional or longitudinal data.
    a. Forecasting
    b. 100-year flood
    c. 130-30 fund
    d. 1921 recession

12. In economics, a _____ or a hard good is a good which does not quickly wear out it yields services or utility over time rather than being completely used up when used once. Most goods are therefore _____s to a certain degree. These are goods that can last for a relatively long time, such as refrigerators, cars, and DVD players.
    a. Durable good
    b. Superior goods
    c. Search good
    d. Luxury good

13. _____ is a term in economics, where demand for one good or service occurs as a result of demand for another. This may occur as the former is a part of production of the second. For example, demand for coal leads to _____ for mining, as coal must be mined for coal to be consumed.
    a. Leontief production function
    b. Derived demand
    c. Days Sales Outstanding
    d. Rate risk

14. In economics, _____ is the ratio of the percent change in one variable to the percent change in another variable. It is a tool for measuring the responsiveness of a function to changes in parameters in a relative way. Commonly analyzed are _____ of substitution, price and wealth.

a. ACEA agreement
b. Elasticity of demand
c. ACCRA Cost of Living Index
d. Elasticity

15. Price _____ is defined as the measure of responsiveness in the quantity demanded for a commodity as a result of change in price of the same commodity. It is a measure of how consumers react to a change in price. In other words, it is percentage change in quantity demanded by the percentage change in price of the same commodity.
   a. ACCRA Cost of Living Index
   b. ACEA agreement
   c. Elasticity of demand
   d. Elasticity

16. _____ in economics and business is the result of an exchange and from that trade we assign a numerical monetary value to a good, service or asset. If Alice trades Bob 4 apples for an orange, the _____ of an orange is 4 apples. Inversely, the _____ of an apple is 1/4 oranges.
   a. Price book
   b. Premium pricing
   c. Price
   d. Price war

17. _____ is defined as the measure of responsiveness in the quantity demanded for a commodity as a result of change in price of the same commodity. It is a measure of how consumers react to a change in price. In other words, it is percentage change in quantity demanded as per the percentage change in price of the same commodity.
   a. Price elasticity of demand
   b. 130-30 fund
   c. 1921 recession
   d. 100-year flood

18. In microeconomics, _____ is the extra revenue that an additional unit of product will bring. It is the additional income from selling one more unit of a good; sometimes equal to price. It can also be described as the change in total revenue/change in number of units sold.
   a. Reservation price
   b. Market demand schedule
   c. Long term
   d. Marginal revenue

19. _____ is the total money received from the sale of any given quantity of output.

The _____ is calculated by taking the price of the sale times the quantity sold, i.e.

_____ = price X quantity.

   a. Market development funds
   b. Ceteris paribus
   c. Small numbers game
   d. Total revenue

20. In neoclassical economics and microeconomics, _____ describes the perfect being a market in which there are many small firms, all producing homogeneous goods. In the short term, such markets are productively inefficient as output will not occur where mc is equal to ac, but allocatively efficient, as output under _____ will always occur where mc is equal to mr, and therefore where mc equals ar. However, in the long term, such markets are both allocatively and productively efficient.
   a. Law of supply
   b. General equilibrium
   c. Perfect competition
   d. Co-operative economics

Chapter 3. Demand Theory

21. In economics, the _____ of demand measures the responsiveness of the demand of a good to the change in the income of the people demanding the good. It is calculated as the ratio of the percent change in demand to the percent change in income. For example, if, in response to a 10% increase in income, the demand of a good increased by 20%, the _____ of demand would be 20%/10% = 2.
    a. AD-IA Model
    b. ACEA agreement
    c. ACCRA Cost of Living Index
    d. Income elasticity

22. In economics, the _____ measures the responsiveness of the demand of a good to the change in the income of the people demanding the good. It is calculated as the ratio of the percent change in demand to the percent change in income. For example, if, in response to a 10% increase in income, the demand of a good increased by 20%, the _____ would be 20%/10% = 2.
    a. Elasticity of substitution
    b. Indifference map
    c. Expenditure minimization problem
    d. Income elasticity of demand

23. _____s is the social science that studies the production, distribution, and consumption of goods and services. The term _____s comes from the Ancient Greek οἰκονομία from οἶκος (oikos, 'house') + νόμος (nomos, 'custom' or 'law'), hence 'rules of the house(hold)'. Current _____ models developed out of the broader field of political economy in the late 19th century, owing to a desire to use an empirical approach more akin to the physical sciences.
    a. Energy economics
    b. Inflation
    c. Economic
    d. Opportunity cost

24. _____, is a branch of economics that applies microeconomic analysis to decision methods of businesses or other management units. As such, it bridges economic theory and economics in practice. It draws heavily from quantitative techniques such as regression analysis and correlation, Lagrangian calculus (linear.)
    a. Club goods
    b. Forward exchange market
    c. Black-Litterman model
    d. Managerial economics

25. _____, commonly known as (electronic marketing) e-commerce or eCommerce, consists of the buying and selling of products or services over electronic systems such as the Internet and other computer networks. The amount of trade conducted electronically has grown extraordinarily with widespread Internet usage. The use of commerce is conducted in this way, spurring and drawing on innovations in electronic funds transfer, supply chain management, Internet marketing, online transaction processing, electronic data interchange (EDI), inventory management systems, and automated data collection systems.
    a. Electronic commerce
    b. Automated Clearing House
    c. Auction software
    d. Electronic Data Interchange

26. The _____ consists of a number of economic theories which describe the nature of the firm, company including its existence, its behaviour, and its relationship with the market.

In simplified terms, the _____ aims to answer these questions:

1. Existence - why do firms emerge, why are not all transactions in the economy mediated over the market?
2. Boundaries - why the boundary between firms and the market is located exactly there? Which transactions are performed internally and which are negotiated on the market?
3. Organization - why are firms structured in such specific way? What is the interplay of formal and informal relationships?

Despite looking simple, these questions are not answered by the established economic theory, which usually views firms as given, and treats them as black boxes without any internal structure.

The First World War period saw a change of emphasis in economic theory away from industry-level analysis which mainly included analysing markets to analysis at the level of the firm, as it became increasingly clear that perfect competition was no longer an adequate model of how firms behaved. Economic theory till then had focussed on trying to understand markets alone and there had been little study on understanding why firms or organisations exist.

a. Policy Ineffectiveness Proposition
b. Khazzoom-Brookes postulate
c. Technology gap
d. Theory of the firm

27. _____ is an economic system in which wealth, and the means of producing wealth, are privately owned. Through _____, the land, labor, and capital are owned, operated, and traded for the purpose of generating profits, without force or fraud, by private individuals either singly or jointly, and investments, distribution, income, production, pricing and supply of goods, commodities and services are determined by voluntary private decision in a market economy. A distinguishing feature of _____ is that each person owns his or her own labor and therefore is allowed to sell the use of it to employers.

a. Socialism for the rich and capitalism for the poor
b. Creative capitalism
c. Late capitalism
d. Capitalism

28. _____ is a broad label that refers to any individuals or households that use goods and services generated within the economy. The concept of a _____ is used in different contexts, so that the usage and significance of the term may vary.

Typically when business people and economists talk of _____s they are talking about person as _____, an aggregated commodity item with little individuality other than that expressed in the buy/not-buy decision.

a. 130-30 fund
b. 100-year flood
c. 1921 recession
d. Consumer

29. In microeconomic theory, an _____ is a graph showing different bundles of goods, each measured as to quantity, between which a consumer is indifferent. That is, at each point on the curve, the consumer has no preference for one bundle over another. In other words, they are all equally preferred.

a. Engel curve
c. Expenditure minimization problem

b. Indifference map
d. Indifference curve

30. In economics, the _____ is the change in consumption resulting from a change in real income.

Another important item that can change is the money income of the consumer. The _____ is the phenomenon observed through changes in purchasing power.

a. Export subsidy
c. Equilibrium wage

b. Inflation hedge
d. Income effect

Chapter 4. Demand Estimation

1. Economics:

    - _____, the desire to own something and the ability to pay for it
    - _____ curve, a graphic representation of a _____ schedule
    - _____ deposit, the money in checking accounts
    - _____ pull theory, the theory that inflation occurs when _____ for goods and services exceeds existing supplies
    - _____ schedule, a table that lists the quantity of a good a person will buy it each different price
    - _____ side economics, the school of economics at believes government spending and tax cuts open economy by raising _____

    a. McKesson ' Robbins scandal
    b. Demand
    c. Production
    d. Variability

2. _____ is a broad label that refers to any individuals or households that use goods and services generated within the economy. The concept of a _____ is used in different contexts, so that the usage and significance of the term may vary.

    Typically when business people and economists talk of _____s they are talking about person as _____, an aggregated commodity item with little individuality other than that expressed in the buy/not-buy decision.

    a. 130-30 fund
    b. 100-year flood
    c. 1921 recession
    d. Consumer

3. _____ consists of the processes a company uses to track and organize its contacts with its current and prospective customers. _____ software is used to support these processes; information about customers and customer interactions can be entered, stored and accessed by employees in different company departments. Typical _____ goals are to improve services provided to customers, and to use customer contact information for targeted marketing.

    a. Technology acceptance model
    b. Market sector
    c. Customer relationship management
    d. Market share

4. In statistics, _____ refers to techniques for the modeling and analysis of numerical data consisting of values of a dependent variable and of one or more independent variables The dependent variable in the regression equation is modeled as a function of the independent variables, corresponding parameters, and an error term. The error term is treated as a random variable.

    a. Regression analysis
    b. 1921 recession
    c. 100-year flood
    d. 130-30 fund

5. A _____ is an expression that compares quantities relative to each other. The most common examples involve two quantities, but any number of quantities can be compared. _____s are represented mathematically by separating each quantity with a colon, for example the _____ 2:3, which is read as the _____ 'two to three'.

    a. 130-30 fund
    b. Y-intercept
    c. 100-year flood
    d. Ratio

Chapter 4. Demand Estimation

6. In statistics, a _____ is, broadly speaking, a statistic whose sampling distribution is a Student's t-distribution. These are a parametric statistic, most frequently used in frequentist statistical hypothesis testing in Student's t-tests, but can be defined and used independently of hypothesis testing.

Broadly speaking, a _____ is any statistic whose sampling distribution is a Student's t-distribution.

a. Path coefficients
c. Standardized coefficients
b. Kurtosis risk
d. T-statistic

7. A _____ is any statistical hypothesis test in which the test statistic follows a Student's t distribution if the null hypothesis is true. It is most commonly applied when the test statistic would follow a normal distribution if the value of a scaling constant were known. When the scaling constant is unknown and is replaced by an estimate based on the data, the test statistic (under certain conditions) follows a Student's t distribution.

a. 100-year flood
c. 1921 recession
b. T-test
d. 130-30 fund

8. In statistics, a _____ is an interval estimate of a population parameter. Instead of estimating the parameter by a single value, an interval likely to include the parameter is given. Thus, _____s are used to indicate the reliability of an estimate.

a. Biostatistics
c. Polynomial regression
b. Confidence interval
d. Logistic regression

9. In mathematics, a _____ is a constant multiplicative factor of a certain object. For example, in the expression $9x^2$, the _____ of x^2 is 9.

The object can be such things as a variable, a vector, a function, etc.

a. 100-year flood
c. 130-30 fund
b. Coefficient
d. 1921 recession

10. In statistics, the _____, R^2 is used in the context of statistical models whose main purpose is the prediction of future outcomes on the basis of other related information. It is the proportion of variability in a data set that is accounted for by the statistical model. It provides a measure of how well future outcomes are likely to be predicted by the model.

a. Feasible generalized least squares
c. DFFITS
b. Partial leverage
d. Coefficient of determination

11. In statistics, _____ indicates the strength and direction of a linear relationship between two random variables. That is in contrast with the usage of the term in colloquial speech, which denotes any relationship, not necessarily linear. In general statistical usage, _____ or co-relation refers to the departure of two random variables from independence.

a. 100-year flood
c. Correlation
b. 1921 recession
d. 130-30 fund

12. In statistics, _____ or explained randomness measures the proportion to which a mathematical model accounts for the variation (= apparent randomness) of a given data set. Often, variation is quantified as variance; then, the more specific term explained variance can be used.

The complementary part of the total variation/randomness/variance is called unexplained or residual.

a. Explained variation
b. ACCRA Cost of Living Index
c. AD-IA Model
d. ACEA agreement

13. In statistics, _____ is a collection of statistical models, and their associated procedures, in which the observed variance is partitioned into components due to different explanatory variables. In its simplest form ANOVA gives a statistical test of whether the means of several groups are all equal, and therefore generalizes Student's two-sample t-test to more than two groups.

There are three conceptual classes of such models:

1. Fixed-effects models assumes that the data came from normal populations which may differ only in their means. (Model 1)
2. Random effects models assume that the data describe a hierarchy of different populations whose differences are constrained by the hierarchy. (Model 2)
3. Mixed-effect models describe situations where both fixed and random effects are present. (Model 3)

In practice, there are several types of ANOVA depending on the number of treatments and the way they are applied to the subjects in the experiment:

- One-way ANOVA is used to test for differences among two or more independent groups. Typically, however, the one-way ANOVA is used to test for differences among at least three groups, since the two-group case can be covered by a T-test (Gossett, 1908.)

a. ACCRA Cost of Living Index
b. ACEA agreement
c. AD-IA Model
d. Analysis of variance

14. The use of the 'F-Statistic' here is not to be confused with 'F-statistics' as used in population study.

In probability theory and statistics, the _____ is a continuous probability distribution. It is also known as Snedecor's F distribution or the Fisher-Snedecor distribution (after R.A. Fisher and George W. Snedecor.)

a. 100-year flood
b. 1921 recession
c. F-distribution
d. 130-30 fund

15. In statistics, _____ has two related meanings:

- the arithmetic _____
- the expected value of a random variable, which is also called the population _____.

Chapter 4. Demand Estimation

It is sometimes stated that the '_____' _____s average. This is incorrect if '_____' is taken in the specific sense of 'arithmetic _____' as there are different types of averages: the _____, median, and mode. Other simple statistical analyses use measures of spread, such as range, interquartile range, or standard deviation. For a real-valued random variable X, the _____ is the expectation of X. Note that not every probability distribution has a defined _____ (or variance); see the Cauchy distribution for an example.

a. 100-year flood
b. 130-30 fund
c. 1921 recession
d. Mean

16. _____ or cross section (of a study population) in statistics and econometrics is a type of one-dimensional data set. _____ refers to data collected by observing many subjects (such as individuals, firms or countries/regions) at the same point of time, or without regard to differences in time. Analysis of _____ usually consists of comparing the differences among the subjects.

a. 1921 recession
b. 100-year flood
c. 130-30 fund
d. Cross-sectional data

17. _____ is a statistical phenomenon in which two or more predictor variables in a multiple regression model are highly correlated. In this situation the coefficient estimates may change erratically in response to small changes in the model or the data. _____ does not reduce the predictive power or reliability of the model as a whole; it only affects calculations regarding individual predictors.

a. Quantile regression
b. Total sum of squares
c. Generalized additive model
d. Multicollinearity

18. _____ is the cross-correlation of a signal with itself. It is a mathematical tool for finding repeating patterns, such as the presence of a periodic signal which has been buried under noise, or identifying the missing fundamental frequency in a signal implied by its harmonic frequencies. It is used frequently in signal processing for analyzing functions or series of values, such as time domain signals.

a. ACCRA Cost of Living Index
b. AD-IA Model
c. ACEA agreement
d. Autocorrelation

19. _____ is the activity of estimating the quantity of a product or service that consumers will purchase. _____ involves techniques including both informal methods, such as educated guesses, and quantitative methods, such as the use of historical sales data or current data from test markets. _____ may be used in making pricing decisions, in assessing future capacity requirements, or in making decisions on whether to enter a new market.

a. Cost price
b. Finance designations
c. Financial Reporting
d. Demand forecasting

20. _____ is the process of estimation in unknown situations. Prediction is a similar, but more general term. Both can refer to estimation of time series, cross-sectional or longitudinal data.

a. Forecasting
b. 1921 recession
c. 100-year flood
d. 130-30 fund

Chapter 4. Demand Estimation

21. _____s is the social science that studies the production, distribution, and consumption of goods and services. The term _____s comes from the Ancient Greek oá¼°κονομῖα from oá¼¶κος (oikos, 'house') + vĺŒµος (nomos, 'custom' or 'law'), hence 'rules of the house(hold)'. Current _____ models developed out of the broader field of political economy in the late 19th century, owing to a desire to use an empirical approach more akin to the physical sciences.
   a. Inflation
   b. Economic
   c. Energy economics
   d. Opportunity cost

22. _____s is concerned with the tasks of developing and applying quantitative or statistical methods to the study and elucidation of economic principles. _____s combines economic theory with statistics to analyze and test economic relationships. Theoretical _____s considers questions about the statistical properties of estimators and tests, while applied _____s is concerned with the application of _____ methods to assess economic theories.
   a. Experimental economics
   b. Evolutionary economics
   c. Economic
   d. Econometric

23. In economics, an _____ is any good or commodity, transported from one country to another country in a legitimate fashion, typically for use in trade. _____ goods or services are provided to foreign consumers by domestic producers. _____ is an important part of international trade.
   a. AD-IA Model
   b. ACEA agreement
   c. ACCRA Cost of Living Index
   d. Export

24. In economics, an _____ is any good (e.g. a commodity) or service brought into one country from another country in a legitimate fashion, typically for use in trade. It is a good that is brought in from another country for sale. _____ goods or services are provided to domestic consumers by foreign producers. An _____ in the receiving country is an export to the sending country.
   a. Economic integration
   b. Incoterms
   c. Import quota
   d. Import

25. In economics, _____ is the ratio of the percent change in one variable to the percent change in another variable. It is a tool for measuring the responsiveness of a function to changes in parameters in a relative way. Commonly analyzed are _____ of substitution, price and wealth.
   a. ACEA agreement
   b. ACCRA Cost of Living Index
   c. Elasticity of demand
   d. Elasticity

26. The _____ is the central banking system of the United States. Created in 1913 by the enactment of the Federal Reserve Act (signed by Woodrow Wilson), it is a quasi-public and quasi-private (government entity with private components) banking system that comprises (1) the presidentially appointed Board of Governors of the _____ in Washington, D.C.; (2) the Federal Open Market Committee; (3) twelve regional Federal Reserve Banks located in major cities throughout the nation acting as fiscal agents for the U.S. Treasury, each with its own nine-member board of directors; (4) numerous other private U.S. member banks, which subscribe to required amounts of non-transferable stock in their regional Federal Reserve Banks; and (5) various advisory councils. Since February 2006, Ben Bernanke has served as the Chairman of the Board of Governors of the _____.
   a. Term auction facility
   b. Monetary Policy Report to the Congress
   c. Federal Reserve System
   d. Federal Reserve System Open Market Account

27. Procter is a surname, and may also refer to:

- Bryan Waller Procter (pseud. Barry Cornwall), English poet
- Goodwin Procter, American law firm
- _____, consumer products multinational

a. Tightness
c. Bucket shop
b. Procter ' Gamble
d. Drawdown

Chapter 5. Demand Forecasting

1. Economics:

   - _____, the desire to own something and the ability to pay for it
   - _____ curve, a graphic representation of a _____ schedule
   - _____ deposit, the money in checking accounts
   - _____ pull theory, the theory that inflation occurs when _____ for goods and services exceeds existing supplies
   - _____ schedule, a table that lists the quantity of a good a person will buy it each different price
   - _____ side economics, the school of economics at believes government spending and tax cuts open economy by raising _____

   a. Demand
   b. McKesson ' Robbins scandal
   c. Production
   d. Variability

2. _____ is the activity of estimating the quantity of a product or service that consumers will purchase. _____ involves techniques including both informal methods, such as educated guesses, and quantitative methods, such as the use of historical sales data or current data from test markets. _____ may be used in making pricing decisions, in assessing future capacity requirements, or in making decisions on whether to enter a new market.
   a. Cost price
   b. Demand forecasting
   c. Financial Reporting
   d. Finance designations

3. In statistics, _____ refers to techniques for the modeling and analysis of numerical data consisting of values of a dependent variable and of one or more independent variables The dependent variable in the regression equation is modeled as a function of the independent variables, corresponding parameters, and an error term. The error term is treated as a random variable.
   a. 130-30 fund
   b. 100-year flood
   c. 1921 recession
   d. Regression analysis

4. _____ is the process of estimation in unknown situations. Prediction is a similar, but more general term. Both can refer to estimation of time series, cross-sectional or longitudinal data.
   a. 130-30 fund
   b. 1921 recession
   c. 100-year flood
   d. Forecasting

5. A _____ is the procedure of systematically acquiring and recording information about the members of a given population. It is a regularly occurring and official count of a particular population. The term is used mostly in connection with national 'population and door to door _____ es' (to be taken every 10 years according to United Nations recommendations), agriculture, and business _____ es.
   a. 1921 recession
   b. 130-30 fund
   c. 100-year flood
   d. Census

6. _____ refers to a business or organization attempting to acquire goods or services to accomplish the goals of the enterprise. Though there are several organizations that attempt to set standards in the _____ process, processes can vary greatly between organizations. Typically the word '_____' is not used interchangeably with the word 'procurement', since procurement typically includes Expediting, Supplier Quality, and Traffic and Logistics (T'L) in addition to _____.

a. 100-year flood
c. 130-30 fund
b. Free port
d. Purchasing

7. A security is a fungible, negotiable instrument representing financial value. _____ are broadly categorized into debt _____; equity _____, e.g., common stocks; and derivative (finance) contracts such as forwards, futures, options and swaps. The company or other entity issuing the security is called the issuer.
a. Settlement risk
c. Pass-Through Certificates
b. Red herring prospectus
d. Securities

8. The U.S. _____ is an independent agency of the United States government which holds primary responsibility for enforcing the federal securities laws and regulating the securities industry, the nation's stock and options exchanges, and other electronic securities markets. The SEC was created by section 4 of the Securities Exchange Act of 1934 (now codified as 15 U.S.C. § 78d and commonly referred to as the 1934 Act.)
a. 130-30 fund
c. Securities and Exchange Commission
b. 100-year flood
d. 1921 recession

9. _____ is a broad label that refers to any individuals or households that use goods and services generated within the economy. The concept of a _____ is used in different contexts, so that the usage and significance of the term may vary.

Typically when business people and economists talk of _____s they are talking about person as _____, an aggregated commodity item with little individuality other than that expressed in the buy/not-buy decision.

a. 130-30 fund
c. 100-year flood
b. 1921 recession
d. Consumer

10. _____ refers to the number of privately owned new homes (technically housing units) on which construction has been started in a given period. This data is divided into three types: single-family houses, townhouses or small condos, and apartment buildings with 5 or more units.

Each apartment unit is considered a single start.

a. 100-year flood
c. 130-30 fund
b. 1921 recession
d. Housing starts

11. In statistics, a _____ is used to analyze a set of data points by creating a series of averages of different subsets of the full data set. So a _____ is not a single number, but it is a set of numbers, each of which is the average of the corresponding subset of a larger set of data points. A simple example is if you had a data set with 100 data points, the first value of the _____ might be the arithmetic mean of data points 1 through 25.
a. Time series
c. Failure rate
b. Type I error
d. Moving average

12. In statistics and image processing, to smooth a data set is to create an approximating function that attempts to capture important patterns in the data, while leaving out noise or other fine-scale structures/rapid phenomena. Many different algorithms are used in _____. One of the most common algorithms is the 'moving average', often used to try to capture important trends in repeated statistical surveys.
   a. X-bar chart
   b. Partial regression plot
   c. Partial residual plot
   d. Smoothing

13. In statistics, _____ is a technique that can be applied to time series data, either to produce smoothed data for presentation, or to make forecasts. The time series data themselves are a sequence of observations. The observed phenomenon may be an essentially random process, or it may be an orderly, but noisy, process.
   a. Innovations vector
   b. Unit root
   c. Autoregressive conditional heteroskedasticity
   d. Exponential smoothing

14. The term _____ refers to economy-wide fluctuations in production or economic activity over several months or years. These fluctuations occur around a long-term growth trend, and typically involve shifts over time between periods of relatively rapid economic growth (expansion or boom), and periods of relative stagnation or decline (contraction or recession.)

These fluctuations are often measured using the growth rate of real gross domestic product.

   a. Tobit model
   b. Business Cycle
   c. Nominal value
   d. Consumer theory

15. In econometrics a _____ is a series which measures the co-movement of many time series. It is used in macroeconomic models.

Formally

$X_t = \Lambda_t F_t + e_t,$

where $F_t = (f_t^T, \ldots, f_{t-q}^T)$ is the vector of lagged factors of the variables in the $T \times N$ matrix X_t, Λ_t are the factor loadings, and e_t is the factor error.

   a. Delta method
   b. Vector autoregression
   c. Multinomial logit
   d. Dynamic factor

16. _____s is the social science that studies the production, distribution, and consumption of goods and services. The term _____s comes from the Ancient Greek οἰκονομία from οἶκος (oikos, 'house') + νόμος (nomos, 'custom' or 'law'), hence 'rules of the house(hold)'. Current _____ models developed out of the broader field of political economy in the late 19th century, owing to a desire to use an empirical approach more akin to the physical sciences.
   a. Inflation
   b. Energy economics
   c. Economic
   d. Opportunity cost

17. A _____ is an economic indicator that reacts slowly to economic changes, and therefore has little predictive value. Generally these types of indicators follow an event; they are historical in nature. For example, in a performance measuring system, profit earned by a business is a _____ as it reflects a historical performance; similarly, improved customer satisfaction is the result of initiatives taken in the past.
   a. Skyscraper Index
   b. Nonfarm payrolls
   c. Bureau of Labor Statistics
   d. Lagging indicator

18. The _____ is a US private, nonprofit research organization dedicated to studying the science and empirics of economics, especially the American economy. It is 'committed to undertaking and disseminating unbiased economic research among public policymakers, business professionals, and the academic community.' It publishes NBER Working Papers and books. The NBER is located in Cambridge, Massachusetts with branch offices in Palo Alto, California, and New York City.
   a. CEFTA
   b. Deutsche Bank
   c. Non-governmental organization
   d. National Bureau of Economic Research

19. An _____ is a statistic about the economy. _____s allow analysis of economic performance and predictions of future performance.

   _____s include various indices, earnings reports, and economic summaries, such as unemployment, housing starts, Consumer Price Index (a measure for inflation), industrial production, bankruptcies, Gross Domestic Product, broadband internet penetration, retail sales, stock market prices, and money supply changes.

   a. Internationalization Index
   b. ACCRA Cost of Living Index
   c. Economic Vulnerability Index
   d. Economic indicator

20. _____s is concerned with the tasks of developing and applying quantitative or statistical methods to the study and elucidation of economic principles. _____s combines economic theory with statistics to analyze and test economic relationships. Theoretical _____s considers questions about the statistical properties of estimators and tests, while applied _____s is concerned with the application of _____ methods to assess economic theories.
   a. Economic
   b. Evolutionary economics
   c. Experimental economics
   d. Econometric

21. _____s are statistical models used in econometrics. An _____ specifies the statistical relationship that is believed to hold between the various economic quantities pertaining a particular economic phenomena under study. An _____ can be derived from a deterministic economic model by allowing for uncertainty or from an economic model which itself is stochastic.
   a. Event study
   b. ACCRA Cost of Living Index
   c. Economic statistics
   d. Econometric model

22. _____ in its literal sense is the process of transformation of local or regional phenomena into global ones. It can be described as a process by which the people of the world are unified into a single society and function together.

This process is a combination of economic, technological, sociocultural and political forces.

a. Globalization
b. Global Cosmopolitanism
c. Helsinki Process on Globalisation and Democracy
d. Globally Integrated Enterprise

23. The _____ is an American economic index intended to estimate future economic activity. It is calculated by The Conference Board, a non-governmental organization, which determines the value of the index from the values of ten key variables. These variables have historically turned downward before a recession and upward before an expansion.

a. Atkinson index
b. Index of dissimilarity
c. Index of diversity
d. Index of leading indicators

24. In economics, _____ are key economic variables that economists used to predict a new phase of the business cycle. A leading indicator is one that changes before the economy does; a lagging indicator is one that changes after the economy has changed. Examples of _____ include stock prices, which often improve or worsen before a similar change in the economy.

a. Medium of exchange
b. Gross domestic product
c. Leading indicators
d. Macroeconomics

25. _____ refers to an action or object coming from outside a system. It is the opposite of endogenous, something generated from within the system.

- In an economic model, an _____ change is one that comes from outside the model and is unexplained by the model. For example, in the simple supply and demand model, a change in consumer tastes or preferences is unexplained by the model and also leads to endogenous changes in demand that lead to changes in the equilibrium price. Put another way, an _____ change involves an alteration of a variable that is autonomous, i.e., unaffected by the workings of the model.

- In linear regression, it means that the variable is independent of all other response values.

- In biology, '_____' refers to an action or object coming from the outside of a system. For example, an _____ contrast agent in medical imaging refers to a liquid injected into the patient intravenously that enhances visibility of a pathology, such as a tumor.

a. AD-IA Model
b. ACCRA Cost of Living Index
c. ACEA agreement
d. Exogenous

26. _____ is an American economist and was the Chairman of the Federal Reserve of the United States from 1987 to 2006. He currently works as a private advisor and providing consulting for firms through his company, Greenspan Associates LLC.

First appointed Federal Reserve chairman by President Ronald Reagan in August 1987, he was reappointed at successive four-year intervals until retiring on January 31, 2006 after the second-longest tenure in the position.

a. Alan Greenspan
b. Adam Smith
c. Adolph Fischer
d. Adolf Hitler

27. A _____ is a place of residence or refuge and comfort. It is usually a place in which an individual or a family can rest and be able to store personal property. Most modern-day households contain sanitary facilities and a means of preparing food.
   a. 1921 recession
   b. Home
   c. 100-year flood
   d. 130-30 fund

28. _____ is a common concept in economics, and gives rise to derived concepts such as consumer debt. Generally _____ is defined by opposition to production. But the precise definition can vary because different schools of economists define production quite differently.
   a. Federal Reserve Bank Notes
   b. Foreclosure data providers
   c. Consumption
   d. Cash or share options

Chapter 6. Production Theory and Estimation

1. _____ is the term denoting either an entrance or changes which are inserted into a system and which activate/modify a process. It is an abstract concept, used in the modeling, system(s) design and system(s) exploitation. It is usually connected with other terms, e.g., _____ field, _____ variable, _____ parameter, _____ value, _____ signal, _____ device and _____ file.
   a. ACCRA Cost of Living Index
   b. ACEA agreement
   c. AD-IA Model
   d. Input

2. In economic models, the _____ time frame assumes no fixed factors of production. Firms can enter or leave the marketplace, and the cost (and availability) of land, labor, raw materials, and capital goods can be assumed to vary. In contrast, in the short-run time frame, certain factors are assumed to be fixed, because there is not sufficient time for them to change.
   a. Price/performance ratio
   b. Productivity world
   c. Diseconomies of scale
   d. Long-run

3. In microeconomics, _____ is quite simply the conversion of inputs into outputs. It is an economic process that uses resources to create a good or service that is suitable for exchange. This can include manufacturing, storing, shipping, and packaging.
   a. Production
   b. Solved
   c. Red Guards
   d. MET

4. In economics, the concept of the _____ refers to the decision-making time frame of a firm in which at least one factor of production is fixed. Costs which are fixed in the _____ have no impact on a firms decisions. For example a firm can raise output by increasing the amount of labour through overtime.
   a. Short-run
   b. Hicks-neutral technical change
   c. Product Pipeline
   d. Productivity model

5. _____s are financial contracts whose values are derived from the value of something else (known as the underlying.) The underlying value on which a _____ is based can be an asset (e.g., commodities, equities (stocks), residential mortgages, commercial real estate, loans, bonds), an index (e.g., interest rates, exchange rates, stock market indices, consumer price index (CPI) -- see inflation _____s), weather conditions bonds or other forms of credit.
   a. Derivative
   b. Second derivative
   c. 130-30 fund
   d. 100-year flood

6. In economics, a _____ is a function that specifies the output of a firm, an industry, or an entire economy for all combinations of inputs. A meta-_____ compares the practice of the existing entities converting inputs X into output y to determine the most efficient practice _____ of the existing entities, whether the most efficient feasible practice production or the most efficient actual practice production. In either case, the maximum output of a technologically-determined production process is a mathematical function of input factors of production.
   a. Short-run
   b. Production function
   c. Constant elasticity of substitution
   d. Post-Fordism

7. In economics, the _____ functional form of production functions is widely used to represent the relationship of an output to inputs. It was proposed by Knut Wicksell (1851-1926), and tested against statistical evidence by Charles Cobb and Paul Douglas in 1900-1928.

Chapter 6. Production Theory and Estimation

For production, the function is

$$Y = AL^{\alpha}K^{\beta},$$

where:

- Y = total production (the monetary value of all goods produced in a year)
- L = labor input
- K = capital input
- A = total factor productivity
- α and β are the output elasticities of labor and capital, respectively. These values are constants determined by available technology.

Output elasticity measures the responsiveness of output to a change in levels of either labor or capital used in production, ceteris paribus. For example if α = 0.15, a 1% increase in labor would lead to approximately a 0.15% increase in output.

a. Growth accounting
c. Cobb-Douglas
b. Social savings
d. Demand-pull theory

8. In economics, _____ is the ratio of the percent change in one variable to the percent change in another variable. It is a tool for measuring the responsiveness of a function to changes in parameters in a relative way. Commonly analyzed are _____ of substitution, price and wealth.

a. Elasticity
c. ACEA agreement
b. Elasticity of demand
d. ACCRA Cost of Living Index

9. In economics, the _____ or marginal physical product is the extra output produced by one more unit of an input (for instance, the difference in output when a firm's labour is increased from five to six units.) Assuming that no other inputs to production change, the _____ of a given input (X) can be expressed as:

_____ = ΔY/ΔX = (the change of Y)/(the change of X.)

-
  - ○
    - Pending approval by Thomas Sowell***

In neoclassical economics, this is the mathematical derivative of the production function.... Note that the 'product' (Y) is typically defined ignoring external costs and benefits.

a. Productive capacity
c. Labor problem
b. Factor prices
d. Marginal product

10. In economics, _____ is the percentage change of output (GDP or revenue for a single firm) divided by the percentage change of an input.

It is calculated as marginal product of an input to its average product. It is a local measure, defined at a point.

a. Inventory turnover ratio
b. Accumulated other comprehensive income
c. Eco commerce
d. Output elasticity

11. The _____ of a variable factor of Production identifies what outputs are possible using various levels of the variable input. This can be displayed in either a chart that lists the output level corresponding to various levels of input, or a graph that summarizes the data into a '_____ curve'. The diagram shows a typical _____ curve. In this example, output increases as more inputs are employed up until point A. The maximum output possible with this Production process is Qm. (If there are other inputs used in the process, they are assumed to be fixed).

a. Total product
b. Convexity
c. Tightness
d. Consequence

12. In economics, _____ refers to how the marginal contribution of a factor of production usually decreases as more of the factor is used. According to this relationship, in a production system with fixed and variable inputs, beyond some point, each additional unit of the variable input yields smaller and smaller increases in output. Conversely, producing one more unit of output costs more and more in variable inputs.

a. Patent troll
b. Derivatives law
c. Community property
d. Diminishing returns

13. In microeconomics, _____ is the extra revenue that an additional unit of product will bring. It is the additional income from selling one more unit of a good; sometimes equal to price. It can also be described as the change in total revenue/change in number of units sold.

a. Reservation price
b. Market demand schedule
c. Long term
d. Marginal revenue

14. The marginal revenue productivity theory of wages, also referred to as the _____ of labor, is the change in total revenue earned by a firm that results from employing one more unit of labor. It is a neoclassical model that determines, under some conditions, the optimal number of workers to employ at an exogenously determined market wage rate.

The _____ of a worker is equal to the product of the marginal product of labor (MP) and the marginal revenue (MR), given by MR×MP = _____.

a. Coal depletion
b. Marginal revenue product
c. Marginal revenue productivity theory of wages
d. Real prices and ideal prices

15. In economics, an _____ is a contour line drawn through the set of points at which the same quantity of output is produced while changing the quantities of two or more inputs. While an indifference curve helps to answer the utility-maximizing problem of consumers, the _____ deals with the cost-minimization problem of producers. _____s are typically drawn on capital-labor graphs, showing the tradeoff between capital and labor in the production function, and the decreasing marginal returns of both inputs.

a. Isoquant
b. Underinvestment employment relationship
c. Economic production quantity
d. Economies of scale

16. In economics, the _____ or the Technical Rate of Substitution (TRS) is the amount by which the quantity of one input has to be reduced ($-\Delta x_2$) when one extra unit of another input is used ($\Delta x_1 = 1$), so that output remains constant ($y = \bar{y}$.)

$$MRTS(x_1, x_2) = \frac{\Delta x_2}{\Delta x_1} = -\frac{MP_1}{MP_2}$$

where MP_1 and MP_2 are the marginal products of input 1 and input 2, respectively.

Along an isoquant, the MRTS shows the rate at which one input (e.g. capital or labor) may be substituted for another, while maintaining the same level of output.

a. Marginal rate of technical substitution
c. Producer surplus
b. Household production function
d. Pork cycle

17. In economics, _____ is the process by which a firm determines the price and output level that returns the greatest profit. There are several approaches to this problem. The total revenue--total cost method relies on the fact that profit equals revenue minus cost, and the marginal revenue--marginal cost method is based on the fact that total profit in a perfectly competitive market reaches its maximum point where marginal revenue equals marginal cost.
a. 100-year flood
c. Profit margin
b. Profit maximization
d. Normal profit

18. A _____ is an object whose consumption increases the utility of the consumer, for which the quantity demanded exceeds the quantity supplied at zero price. _____s are usually modeled as having diminishing marginal utility. The first individual purchase has high utility; the second has less.
a. Good
c. Pie method
b. Merit good
d. Composite good

19. _____ in economics and business is the result of an exchange and from that trade we assign a numerical monetary value to a good, service or asset. If Alice trades Bob 4 apples for an orange, the _____ of an orange is 4 apples. Inversely, the _____ of an apple is 1/4 oranges.
a. Price book
c. Premium pricing
b. Price
d. Price war

20. _____ is a common concept in economics, and gives rise to derived concepts such as consumer debt. Generally _____ is defined by opposition to production. But the precise definition can vary because different schools of economists define production quite differently.
a. Consumption
c. Foreclosure data providers
b. Federal Reserve Bank Notes
d. Cash or share options

21. In production, returns to scale refers to changes in output subsequent to a proportional change in all inputs (where all inputs increase by a constant factor.) If output increases by that same proportional change then there are _____ If output increases by less than that proportional change, there are decreasing returns to scale (DRS.)

a. Lexicographic preferences
b. Long term
c. Consumer sovereignty
d. Constant returns to scale

22. In calculus, a function f defined on a subset of the real numbers with real values is called _____, if for all x and y such that x >≤ y one has f(x) >≤ f(y), so f preserves the order. In layman's terms, the sign of the slope is always positive (the curve tending upwards) or zero (i.e., non-decreasing, or asymptotic, or depicted as a horizontal, flat line) Likewise, a function is called monotonically decreasing (non-increasing) if, whenever x >≤ y, then f(x) >≥ f(y), so it reverses the order.
a. 130-30 fund
b. 1921 recession
c. Monotonic
d. 100-year flood

23. In economics, _____ and economies of scale are related terms that describe what happens as the scale of production increases. They are different terms and should not be used interchangeably.

_____ refers to a technical property of production that examines changes in output subsequent to a proportional change in all inputs (where all inputs increase by a constant factor.)

a. Customer equity
b. Returns to scale
c. Necessity good
d. Constant returns to scale

24. _____ in its literal sense is the process of transformation of local or regional phenomena into global ones. It can be described as a process by which the people of the world are unified into a single society and function together.

This process is a combination of economic, technological, sociocultural and political forces.

a. Helsinki Process on Globalisation and Democracy
b. Globally Integrated Enterprise
c. Globalization
d. Global Cosmopolitanism

25. The process of _____ involves the introduction of a good or service that is new or substantially improved. This includes, but is not limited to, improvements in functional characteristics, technical abilities, or ease of use.
a. Refusal to deal
b. Microcap stock
c. Dogs of the Dow
d. Product innovation

26. _____ is a comparative concept of the ability and performance of a firm, sub-sector or country to sell and supply goods and/or services in a given market. Although widely used in economics and business management, the usefulness of the concept, particularly in the context of national _____, is vigorously disputed by economists, such as Paul Krugman .

The term may also be applied to markets, where it is used to refer to the extent to which the market structure may be regarded as perfectly competitive.

a. Debt moratorium
b. Competitiveness
c. Quota share
d. Countervailing duties

27. The _____ is an important selective, mainly private, international organization designed by its founders to supervise and liberalize international trade. The organization officially commenced on 1 January 1995, under the Marrakesh Agreement, succeeding the 1947 General Agreement on Tariffs and Trade (GATT.)

Chapter 6. Production Theory and Estimation

The _____ deals with regulation of trade between participating countries; it provides a framework for negotiating and formalising trade agreements, and a dispute resolution process aimed at enforcing participants' adherence to _____ agreements which are signed by representatives of member governments and ratified by their parliaments.

a. 2009 G-20 London summit protests
b. Bio-energy village
c. Backus-Kehoe-Kydland consumption correlation puzzle
d. World Trade Organization

28. The _____ is the official currency of 16 of the 27 member states of the European Union (EU.) The states, known collectively as the Eurozone, are Austria, Belgium, Cyprus, Finland, France, Germany, Greece, Ireland, Italy, Luxembourg, Malta, the Netherlands, Portugal, Slovakia, Slovenia, and Spain. The currency is also used in a further five European countries, with and without formal agreements and is consequently used daily by some 327 million Europeans.

a. Euro
b. Import and Export Price Indices
c. IRS Code 3401
d. Equity capital market

29. A _____, reserve bank, or monetary authority is the entity responsible for the monetary policy of a country or of a group of member states. It is a bank that can lend money to other banks in times of need. Its primary responsibility is to maintain the stability of the national currency and money supply, but more active duties include controlling subsidized-loan interest rates, and acting as a lender of last resort to the banking sector during times of financial crisis (private banks often being integral to the national financial system.)

a. 100-year flood
b. 130-30 fund
c. 1921 recession
d. Central Bank

30. The _____ is one of the world's most important central banks, responsible for monetary policy covering the 16 member States of the Eurozone. It was established by the European Union (EU) in 1998 with its headquarters in Frankfurt, Germany.

The predecessor to the _____ was the European Monetary Institute .

a. European Central Bank
b. AD-IA Model
c. ACCRA Cost of Living Index
d. ACEA agreement

31. Procter is a surname, and may also refer to:

- Bryan Waller Procter (pseud. Barry Cornwall), English poet
- Goodwin Procter, American law firm
- _____, consumer products multinational

a. Drawdown
b. Tightness
c. Procter ' Gamble
d. Bucket shop

Chapter 7. Cost Theory and Estimation

1. An _____ is an easy accounted cost, such as wage, rent and materials. It can be transacted in the form of money payment and is lost directly, as opposed to monetary implicit costs.
   a. Average variable cost
   b. Explicit cost
   c. Average fixed cost
   d. Inventory valuation

2. In economics, an _____ occurs when one foregoes an alternative action but does not make an actual payment. (For instance, the explicit cost of a night at the movies includes the moviegoer's ticket and soda, but the _____ includes the pay he would have earned if he had chosen to work instead.) _____s are related to forgone benefits of any single transaction.
   a. Overnight trade
   b. Implicit cost
   c. External sector
   d. Ostrich strategy

3. _____ is a term used in accounting, economics and finance to spread the cost of an asset over the span of several years.

In simple words we can say that _____ is the reduction in the value of an asset due to usage, passage of time, wear and tear, technological outdating or obsolescence, depletion, inadequacy, rot, rust, decay or other such factors.

In accounting, _____ is a term used to describe any method of attributing the historical or purchase cost of an asset across its useful life, roughly corresponding to normal wear and tear.

   a. Depreciation
   b. Salvage value
   c. Net income per employee
   d. Historical cost

4. _____s is the social science that studies the production, distribution, and consumption of goods and services. The term _____s comes from the Ancient Greek οἰκονομία from οἶκος (oikos, 'house') + νόμος (nomos, 'custom' or 'law'), hence 'rules of the house(hold)'. Current _____ models developed out of the broader field of political economy in the late 19th century, owing to a desire to use an empirical approach more akin to the physical sciences.
   a. Energy economics
   b. Inflation
   c. Opportunity cost
   d. Economic

5. The _____ of a decision depends on both the cost of the alternative chosen and the benefit that the best alternative would have provided if chosen. _____ differs from accounting cost because it includes opportunity cost.
   a. Isocost
   b. Epstein-Zin preferences
   c. Inventory analysis
   d. Economic cost

6. In economics and finance, _____ is the change in total cost that arises when the quantity produced changes by one unit. It is the cost of producing one more unit of a good. Mathematically, the _____ function is expressed as the first derivative of the total cost (TC) function with respect to quantity (Q.)
   a. Khozraschyot
   b. Quality costs
   c. Variable cost
   d. Marginal cost

7. _____ or economic opportunity loss is the value of the next best alternative foregone as the result of making a decision. _____ analysis is an important part of a company's decision-making processes but is not treated as an actual cost in any financial statement. The next best thing that a person can engage in is referred to as the _____ of doing the best thing and ignoring the next best thing to be done.

a. Economic ideology
b. Economic
c. Industrial organization
d. Opportunity cost

8. In economics, the concept of the _____ refers to the decision-making time frame of a firm in which at least one factor of production is fixed. Costs which are fixed in the _____ have no impact on a firms decisions. For example a firm can raise output by increasing the amount of labour through overtime.
a. Short-run
b. Product Pipeline
c. Productivity model
d. Hicks-neutral technical change

9. In economics and business decision-making, _____ are costs that cannot be recovered once they have been incurred. _____ are sometimes contrasted with variable costs, which are the costs that will change due to the proposed course of action, and prospective costs which are costs that will be incurred if an action is taken.

In traditional microeconomic theory, only variable costs are relevant to a decision.

a. Halo effect
b. Sunk costs
c. Hyperbolic discounting
d. Post-purchase rationalization

10. In economics, and cost accounting, _____ describes the total economic cost of production and is made up of variable costs, which vary according to the quantity of a good produced and include inputs such as labor and raw materials, plus fixed costs, which are independent of the quantity of a good produced and include inputs (capital) that cannot be varied in the short term, such as buildings and machinery. _____ in economics includes the total opportunity cost of each factor of production in addition to fixed and variable costs.

The rate at which _____ changes as the amount produced changes is called marginal cost.

a. 130-30 fund
b. 1921 recession
c. 100-year flood
d. Total cost

11. In economics, _____ are business expenses that are not dependent on the activities of the business They tend to be time-related, such as salaries or rents being paid per month. This is in contrast to variable costs, which are volume-related (and are paid per quantity.)

In management accounting, _____ are defined as expenses that do not change in proportion to the activity of a business, within the relevant period or scale of production.

a. Cost-Volume-Profit Analysis
b. Quality costs
c. Cost of poor quality
d. Fixed costs

12. _____s are expenses that change in proportion to the activity of a business. In other words, _____ is the sum of marginal costs. It can also be considered normal costs.
a. Quality costs
b. Cost allocation
c. Cost-Volume-Profit Analysis
d. Variable cost

13. _____ is an economics term used to describe the total fixed costs (TFC) divided by the quantity (Q) of units produced.

$$AFC = \frac{TFC}{Q}$$

_____ is a per-unit measure of fixed costs. As the total number of goods produced increases, the _____ decreases because the same amount of fixed costs are being spread over a larger number of units.

a. Average variable cost
c. Explicit cost

b. Inventory valuation
d. Average fixed cost

14. _____ is an economics term to describe a firms variable costs (labor, electricity, etc.) divided by the quantity (Q) of total units of output.

$$AVC = \frac{TVC}{Q}$$

Where:

- TVC = Total Variable Cost
- _____ = Average variable cost
- Q = Quantity of Units Produced

_____ plus average fixed cost equals average total cost:

_____ + AFC = ATC.

a. Explicit cost
c. Inventory valuation

b. Average fixed cost
d. Average variable cost

15. In economics, a _____ is a graph of the costs of production as a function of total quantity produced. In a free market economy, productively efficient firms use these curves to find the optimal point of production, where they make the most profits. There are a few different types of _____s, each relevant to a different area of economics.
a. Phillips curve
c. Demand curve

b. Cost curve
d. Kuznets curve

16. In economic models, the _____ time frame assumes no fixed factors of production. Firms can enter or leave the marketplace, and the cost (and availability) of land, labor, raw materials, and capital goods can be assumed to vary. In contrast, in the short-run time frame, certain factors are assumed to be fixed, because there is not sufficient time for them to change.
a. Long-run
c. Diseconomies of scale

b. Price/performance ratio
d. Productivity world

Chapter 7. Cost Theory and Estimation

17. In economics, _____ is equal to total cost divided by the number of goods produced (the output quantity, Q.) It is also equal to the sum of average variable costs (total variable costs divided by Q) plus average fixed costs (total fixed costs divided by Q.) _____s may be dependent on the time period considered (increasing production may be expensive or impossible in the short term, for example.)
   a. Explicit cost
   b. Average variable cost
   c. Average cost
   d. Average fixed cost

18. _____, in microeconomics, are the cost advantages that a business obtains due to expansion. They are factors that cause a producere;s average cost per unit to fall as scale is increased. _____ is a long run concept and refers to reductions in unit cost as the size of a facility, or scale, increases.
   a. Underinvestment employment relationship
   b. Economic production quantity
   c. Isoquant
   d. Economies of scale

19. _____ are conceptually similar to economies of scale. Whereas economies of scale primarily refer to efficiencies associated with supply-side changes, such as increasing or decreasing the scale of production, of a single product type, _____ refer to efficiencies primarily associated with demand-side changes, such as increasing or decreasing the scope of marketing and distribution, of different types of products. _____ are one of the main reasons for such marketing strategies as product bundling, product lining, and family branding.
   a. Economies of scope
   b. Economies of scale
   c. Isoquant
   d. Economic production quantity

20. _____ is the term denoting either an entrance or changes which are inserted into a system and which activate/modify a process. It is an abstract concept, used in the modeling, system(s) design and system(s) exploitation. It is usually connected with other terms, e.g., _____ field, _____ variable, _____ parameter, _____ value, _____ signal, _____ device and _____ file.
   a. ACEA agreement
   b. AD-IA Model
   c. ACCRA Cost of Living Index
   d. Input

21. _____ is subcontracting a process, such as product design or manufacturing, to a third-party company. The decision to outsource is often made in the interest of lowering cost or making better use of time and energy costs, redirecting or conserving energy directed at the competencies of a particular business, or to make more efficient use of land, labor, capital, (information) technology and resources. _____ became part of the business lexicon during the 1980s.
   a. Outsourcing
   b. Electronic business
   c. Averch-Johnson effect
   d. Additional Funds Needed

22. _____ to the arrival of new individuals into a habitat or population. It is a biological concept and is important in population ecology, differentiated from emigration and migration.

   _____ is a modern phenomenon.

   a. Immigration
   b. ACCRA Cost of Living Index
   c. AD-IA Model
   d. ACEA agreement

Chapter 7. Cost Theory and Estimation

23. _____ or human capital flight is a large emigration of individuals with technical skills or knowledge, normally due to conflict, lack of opportunity, political instability, or health risks. _____ is usually regarded as an economic cost, since emigrants usually take with them the fraction of value of their training sponsored by the government. It is a parallel of capital flight which refers to the same movement of financial capital.

a. Brain drain
b. 130-30 fund
c. 100-year flood
d. 1921 recession

24. The break-even point for a product is the point where total revenue received equals the total costs associated with the sale of the product (TR=TC.) A break-even point is typically calculated in order for businesses to determine if it would be profitable to sell a proposed product, as opposed to attempting to modify an existing product instead so it can be made lucrative. _____ can also be used to analyse the potential profitability of an expenditure in a sales-based business.

a. Competitor indexing
b. Break even analysis
c. Price
d. Flat rate

25. The _____ consists of a number of economic theories which describe the nature of the firm, company including its existence, its behaviour, and its relationship with the market.

In simplified terms, the _____ aims to answer these questions:

1. Existence - why do firms emerge, why are not all transactions in the economy mediated over the market?
2. Boundaries - why the boundary between firms and the market is located exactly there? Which transactions are performed internally and which are negotiated on the market?
3. Organization - why are firms structured in such specific way? What is the interplay of formal and informal relationships?

Despite looking simple, these questions are not answered by the established economic theory, which usually views firms as given, and treats them as black boxes without any internal structure.

The First World War period saw a change of emphasis in economic theory away from industry-level analysis which mainly included analysing markets to analysis at the level of the firm, as it became increasingly clear that perfect competition was no longer an adequate model of how firms behaved. Economic theory till then had focussed on trying to understand markets alone and there had been little study on understanding why firms or organisations exist.

a. Policy Ineffectiveness Proposition
b. Khazzoom-Brookes postulate
c. Technology gap
d. Theory of the firm

26. _____, in managerial economics is a form of cost accounting. It is a simplified model, useful for elementary instruction and for short-run decisions.

Cost-volume-profit (CVP) analysis expands the use of information provided by breakeven analysis.

a. Marginal cost
b. Transaction cost
c. Psychic cost
d. Cost-volume-profit analysis

Chapter 7. Cost Theory and Estimation
49

27. In cost-volume-profit analysis, a form of management accounting, _____ is the marginal profit per unit sale. It is a useful quantity in carrying out various calculations, and can be used as a measure of operating leverage.

The Total _____ is Total Revenue (TR, or Sales) minus Total Variable Cost (TVC):

TContribution margin = TR >− TVC

The Unit _____ (C) is Unit Revenue (Price, P) minus Unit Variable Cost (V):

C = P >− V

The _____ Ratio is the percentage of Contribution over Total Revenue, which can be calculated from the unit contribution over unit price or total contribution over Total Revenue:

For instance, if the price is $10 and the unit variable cost is $2, then the unit _____ is $8, and the _____ ratio is $8/$10 = 80%.

- a. 100-year flood
- c. Contribution margin
- b. 130-30 fund
- d. 1921 recession

28. _____ is a branch of applied mathematics that is used in the social sciences (most notably economics), biology, engineering, political science, international relations, computer science, and philosophy. _____ attempts to mathematically capture behavior in strategic situations, in which an individual's success in making choices depends on the choices of others. While initially developed to analyze competitions in which one individual does better at another's expense (zero sum games), it has been expanded to treat a wide class of interactions, which are classified according to several criteria.
- a. Game theory
- c. Proper equilibrium
- b. Discriminatory price auction
- d. Dollar auction

29. The Organization of the Petroleum Exporting Countries is a cartel of twelve countries made up of Algeria, Angola, Ecuador, Iran, Iraq, Kuwait, Libya, Nigeria, Qatar, Saudi Arabia, the United Arab Emirates, and Venezuela. The cartel has maintained its headquarters in Vienna since 1965, and hosts regular meetings among the oil ministers of its Member Countries. Indonesia withdrew its membership in _____ in 2008 after it became a net importer of oil, but stated it would likely return if it became a net exporter in the world.
- a. ACCRA Cost of Living Index
- c. AD-IA Model
- b. ACEA agreement
- d. OPEC

30. The _____ is a measure of how revenue growth translates into growth in operating income. It is a measure of leverage, and of how risky (volatile) a company's operating income is.

There are various measures of _____, which can be interpreted analogously to financial leverage.

Chapter 7. Cost Theory and Estimation

a. Operating margin
b. Invested Capital
c. Upside potential ratio
d. Operating leverage

31. In statistics, _____ refers to techniques for the modeling and analysis of numerical data consisting of values of a dependent variable and of one or more independent variables The dependent variable in the regression equation is modeled as a function of the independent variables, corresponding parameters, and an error term. The error term is treated as a random variable.

a. 1921 recession
b. 130-30 fund
c. 100-year flood
d. Regression analysis

32. Procter is a surname, and may also refer to:

- Bryan Waller Procter (pseud. Barry Cornwall), English poet
- Goodwin Procter, American law firm
- _____, consumer products multinational

a. Procter ' Gamble
b. Drawdown
c. Tightness
d. Bucket shop

33. In microeconomics, _____ is quite simply the conversion of inputs into outputs. It is an economic process that uses resources to create a good or service that is suitable for exchange. This can include manufacturing, storing, shipping, and packaging.

a. Production
b. MET
c. Red Guards
d. Solved

34. The _____ is a US private, nonprofit research organization dedicated to studying the science and empirics of economics, especially the American economy. It is 'committed to undertaking and disseminating unbiased economic research among public policymakers, business professionals, and the academic community.' It publishes NBER Working Papers and books. The NBER is located in Cambridge, Massachusetts with branch offices in Palo Alto, California, and New York City.

a. CEFTA
b. National Bureau of Economic Research
c. Non-governmental organization
d. Deutsche Bank

35. The _____ includes the global processes of exploration, extraction, refining, transporting (often by oil tankers and pipelines), and marketing petroleum products. The largest volume products of the industry are fuel oil and gasoline (petrol.) Petroleum is also the raw material for many chemical products, including pharmaceuticals, solvents, fertilizers, pesticides, and plastics.

a. 1921 recession
b. 130-30 fund
c. 100-year flood
d. Petroleum industry

Chapter 8. Market Structure: Perfect Competition, Monopoly, and Monopolistic Competition

1. In economics, _____ describes the state of a market with respect to competition.

   - Perfect competition, in which the market consists of a very large number of firms producing a homogeneous product.
   - Monopolistic competition where there are a large number of independent firms which have a very small proportion of the market share.
   - Oligopoly, in which a market is dominated by a small number of firms which own more than 40% of the market share.
   - Oligopsony, a market dominated by many sellers and a few buyers.
   - Monopoly, where there is only one provider of a product or service.
   - Natural monopoly, a monopoly in which economies of scale cause efficiency to increase continuously with the size of the firm. A firm is a natural monopoly if it is able to serve the entire market demand at a lower cost than any combination of two or more smaller, more specialized firms.
   - Monopsony, when there is only one buyer in a market.

   The imperfectly competitive structure is quite identical to the realistic market conditions where some monopolistic competitors, monopolists, oligopolists, and duopolists exist and dominate the market conditions. The elements of _____ include the number and size distribution of firms, entry conditions, and the extent of differentiation.

   These somewhat abstract concerns tend to determine some but not all details of a specific concrete market system where buyers and sellers actually meet and commit to trade.

   a. Labour economics
   c. Monopolistic competition

   b. Human capital
   d. Market structure

2. In economic theory, _____ is the competitive situation in any market where the conditions necessary for perfect competition are not satisfied. It is a market structure that does not meet the conditions of perfect competition.

   Forms of _____ include:

   - Monopoly, in which there is only one seller of a good.
   - Oligopoly, in which there is a small number of sellers.
   - Monopolistic competition, in which there are many sellers producing highly differentiated goods.
   - Monopsony, in which there is only one buyer of a good.
   - Oligopsony, in which there is a small number of buyers.

   There may also be _____ in markets due to buyers or sellers lacking information about prices and the goods being traded.

   There may also be _____ due to a time lag in a market.

   a. AD-IA Model
   c. ACEA agreement

   b. ACCRA Cost of Living Index
   d. Imperfect competition

3. _____ is a common market structure where many competing producers sell products that are differentiated from one another (ie. the products are substitutes, but are not exactly alike.) Many markets are monopolistically competitive, common examples include the markets for restaurants, cereal, clothing, shoes and service industries in large cities.

Chapter 8. Market Structure: Perfect Competition, Monopoly, and Monopolistic Competition

a. Perfect competition
b. Mathematical economics
c. Monopolistic competition
d. Financial crisis

4. In economics, a _____ exists when a specific individual or enterprise has sufficient control over a particular product or service to determine significantly the terms on which other individuals shall have access to it. Monopolies are thus characterized by a lack of economic competition for the good or service that they provide and a lack of viable substitute goods. The verb 'monopolize' refers to the process by which a firm gains persistently greater market share than what is expected under perfect competition.

a. 130-30 fund
b. 100-year flood
c. 1921 recession
d. Monopoly

5. An _____ is a market form in which a market or industry is dominated by a small number of sellers (oligopolists.) Because there are few participants in this type of market, each oligopolist is aware of the actions of the others. The decisions of one firm influence, and are influenced by, the decisions of other firms.

a. ACCRA Cost of Living Index
b. Oligopsony
c. ACEA agreement
d. Oligopoly

6. In neoclassical economics and microeconomics, _____ describes the perfect being a market in which there are many small firms, all producing homogeneous goods. In the short term, such markets are productively inefficient as output will not occur where mc is equal to ac, but allocatively efficient, as output under _____ will always occur where mc is equal to mr, and therefore where mc equals ar. However, in the long term, such markets are both allocatively and productively efficient.

a. Co-operative economics
b. Perfect competition
c. General equilibrium
d. Law of supply

7. _____ in economics and business is the result of an exchange and from that trade we assign a numerical monetary value to a good, service or asset. If Alice trades Bob 4 apples for an orange, the _____ of an orange is 4 apples. Inversely, the _____ of an apple is 1/4 oranges.

a. Price war
b. Premium pricing
c. Price book
d. Price

8. Monopoly power is an example of market failure which occurs when one or more of the participants has the ability to influence the price or other outcomes in some general or specialized market. The most commonly discussed form of market power is that of a monopoly, but other forms such as monopsony, and more moderate versions of these two extremes, exist. Market participants that have market power are sometimes referred to as 'price makers', while those without are sometimes called '_____'.

a. Market power
b. Price takers
c. Market concentration
d. Monopolization

9. A _____ is a public market for the trading of company stock and derivatives at an agreed price; these are securities listed on a stock exchange as well as those only traded privately.

The size of the world _____ was estimated at about $36.6 trillion US at the beginning of October 2008 . The total world derivatives market has been estimated at about $791 trillion face or nominal value, 11 times the size of the entire world economy.

Chapter 8. Market Structure: Perfect Competition, Monopoly, and Monopolistic Competition 53

a. Stock Market
c. Adam Smith
b. Adolph Fischer
d. Adolf Hitler

10. In economics, the concept of the _____ refers to the decision-making time frame of a firm in which at least one factor of production is fixed. Costs which are fixed in the _____ have no impact on a firms decisions. For example a firm can raise output by increasing the amount of labour through overtime.
   a. Productivity model
   c. Product Pipeline
   b. Hicks-neutral technical change
   d. Short-run

11. In economics, the _____ is an economic law that states that consumers buy more of a good when its price decreases and less when its price increases.

There are certain goods which do not follow this law. These include Veblen and Giffen goods

   a. Law of demand
   c. Market failure
   b. Financial crisis
   d. Georgism

12. Economics:

   - _____,the desire to own something and the ability to pay for it
   - _____ curve,a graphic representation of a _____ schedule
   - _____ deposit, the money in checking accounts
   - _____ pull theory,the theory that inflation occurs when _____ for goods and services exceeds existing supplies
   - _____ schedule,a table that lists the quantity of a good a person will buy it each different price
   - _____ side economics,the school of economics at believes government spending and tax cuts open economy by raising _____

   a. Production
   c. Demand
   b. Variability
   d. McKesson ' Robbins scandal

13. In economic models, the _____ time frame assumes no fixed factors of production. Firms can enter or leave the marketplace, and the cost (and availability) of land, labor, raw materials, and capital goods can be assumed to vary. In contrast, in the short-run time frame, certain factors are assumed to be fixed, because there is not sufficient time for them to change.
   a. Productivity world
   c. Long-run
   b. Diseconomies of scale
   d. Price/performance ratio

14. The _____ is a term used for industries primarily concerned with the design or manufacture of clothing as well as the distribution and use of textiles.

Prior to the manufacturing processes were mechanized, textiles were produced in the home, and excess sold for extra money. Most cloth was made from either wool, cotton, or flax, depending on the era and location.

54   Chapter 8. Market Structure: Perfect Competition, Monopoly, and Monopolistic Competition

   a. 130-30 fund
   b. 100-year flood
   c. Textile industry
   d. Textile manufacture during the Industrial Revolution

15. _____ in its literal sense is the process of transformation of local or regional phenomena into global ones. It can be described as a process by which the people of the world are unified into a single society and function together.

This process is a combination of economic, technological, sociocultural and political forces.

   a. Globally Integrated Enterprise
   b. Global Cosmopolitanism
   c. Helsinki Process on Globalisation and Democracy
   d. Globalization

16. In economics and finance, _____ is the change in total cost that arises when the quantity produced changes by one unit. It is the cost of producing one more unit of a good. Mathematically, the _____ function is expressed as the first derivative of the total cost (TC) function with respect to quantity (Q.)
   a. Khozraschyot
   b. Marginal cost
   c. Variable cost
   d. Quality costs

17. _____ is sometimes referred to as _____, actually it means Economic Monetary Union.

First ideas of an economic and monetary union in Europe were raised well before establishing the European Communities. For example, already in the League of Nations, Gustav Stresemann asked in 1929 for a European currency (Link) against the background of an increased economic division due to a number of new nation states in Europe after WWI.

   a. Euro Interbank Offered Rate
   b. European Monetary System
   c. Exchange rate mechanism
   d. European Monetary Union

18. The _____ is an economic and political union of 27 member states, located primarily in Europe. It was established by the Treaty of Maastricht on 1 November 1993, upon the foundations of the pre-existing European Economic Community. With a population of almost 500 million, the _____ generates an estimated 30% share (US$18.4 trillion in 2008) of the nominal gross world product.
   a. European Union
   b. European Court of Justice
   c. ACEA agreement
   d. ACCRA Cost of Living Index

19. In finance, the _____s between two currencies specifies how much one currency is worth in terms of the other. It is the value of a foreign natione;s currency in terms of the home natione;s currency. For example an _____ of 102 Japanese yen to the United States dollar means that JPY 102 is worth the same as USD 1.
   a. ACCRA Cost of Living Index
   b. Interbank market
   c. ACEA agreement
   d. Exchange rate

20. _____ is a type of trade policy that allows traders to act and transact without interference from government. Thus, the policy permits trading partners mutual gains from trade, with goods and services produced according to the theory of comparative advantage.

Under a _____ policy, prices are a reflection of true supply and demand, and are the sole determinant of resource allocation.

Chapter 8. Market Structure: Perfect Competition, Monopoly, and Monopolistic Competition

a. 1921 recession
c. 130-30 fund
b. 100-year flood
d. Free Trade

21. An economic and _____ is a single market with a common currency. It is to be distinguished from a mere currency union, which does not involve a single market. This is the fifth stage of economic integration.
   a. Monetary Union
   c. Free trade zone
   b. Commercial invoice
   d. Customs union

22. The _____ is a trilateral trade bloc in North America created by the governments of the United States, Canada, and Mexico. The agreement creating the trade bloc came into force on January 1, 1994. It superseded the Canada-United States Free Trade Agreement between the U.S. and Canada.
   a. Federal Reserve Bank Notes
   c. Case-Shiller Home Price Indices
   b. North American Free Trade Agreement
   d. Demand-side technologies

23. _____ is a term used in accounting relating to the increase in value of an asset. In this sense it is the reverse of depreciation, which measures the fall in value of assets over their normal life-time.

_____ is a rise of a currency in a floating exchange rate.

   a. ACCRA Cost of Living Index
   c. AD-IA Model
   b. ACEA agreement
   d. Appreciation

24. _____ is a term used in accounting, economics and finance to spread the cost of an asset over the span of several years.

In simple words we can say that _____ is the reduction in the value of an asset due to usage, passage of time, wear and tear, technological outdating or obsolescence, depletion, inadequacy, rot, rust, decay or other such factors.

In accounting, _____ is a term used to describe any method of attributing the historical or purchase cost of an asset across its useful life, roughly corresponding to normal wear and tear.

   a. Depreciation
   c. Salvage value
   b. Net income per employee
   d. Historical cost

25. The _____ consists of a number of economic theories which describe the nature of the firm, company including its existence, its behaviour, and its relationship with the market.

Chapter 8. Market Structure: Perfect Competition, Monopoly, and Monopolistic Competition

In simplified terms, the _____ aims to answer these questions:

1. Existence - why do firms emerge, why are not all transactions in the economy mediated over the market?
2. Boundaries - why the boundary between firms and the market is located exactly there? Which transactions are performed internally and which are negotiated on the market?
3. Organization - why are firms structured in such specific way? What is the interplay of formal and informal relationships?

Despite looking simple, these questions are not answered by the established economic theory, which usually views firms as given, and treats them as black boxes without any internal structure.

The First World War period saw a change of emphasis in economic theory away from industry-level analysis which mainly included analysing markets to analysis at the level of the firm, as it became increasingly clear that perfect competition was no longer an adequate model of how firms behaved. Economic theory till then had focussed on trying to understand markets alone and there had been little study on understanding why firms or organisations exist.

a. Technology gap
b. Theory of the firm
c. Khazzoom-Brookes postulate
d. Policy Ineffectiveness Proposition

26. In economics, a firm is said to reap _____s when a lack of viable market competition allows it to set its prices above the equilibrium price for a good or service without losing profits to competitors. _____ is a type of economic profit, that is, it is a profit greater than the normal profit that is typical in a perfectly competitive industry. The resulting price is known as the monopoly price.

a. Cleanup clause
b. First-price sealed-bid auction
c. Monopoly profit
d. Borrowing base

27. The _____ is an important selective, mainly private, international organization designed by its founders to supervise and liberalize international trade. The organization officially commenced on 1 January 1995, under the Marrakesh Agreement, succeeding the 1947 General Agreement on Tariffs and Trade (GATT.)

The _____ deals with regulation of trade between participating countries; it provides a framework for negotiating and formalising trade agreements, and a dispute resolution process aimed at enforcing participants' adherence to _____ agreements which are signed by representatives of member governments and ratified by their parliaments.

a. Backus-Kehoe-Kydland consumption correlation puzzle
b. 2009 G-20 London summit protests
c. Bio-energy village
d. World Trade Organization

28. In economics _____ is defined as the sum of private and external costs. Economic theorists ascribe individual decision-making to a calculation costs and benefits. Rational choice theory assumes that individuals only consider their own private costs when making decisions, not the costs that may be borne by others.

Chapter 8. Market Structure: Perfect Competition, Monopoly, and Monopolistic Competition   57

a. Cost-Volume-Profit Analysis
b. Khozraschyot
c. Social cost
d. Psychic cost

29. The _____ is an independent agency of the United States government, established in 1914 by the _____ Act. Its principal mission is the promotion of 'consumer protection' and the elimination and prevention of what regulators perceive to be harmfully 'anti-competitive' business practices, such as coercive monopoly.

The _____ Act was one of President Wilson's major acts against trusts.

a. 100-year flood
b. 130-30 fund
c. 1921 recession
d. Federal Trade Commission

30. _____ is an equity (stock) exchange located at 11 Wall Street in lower Manhattan, New York, USA. It is the largest stock exchange in the world by dollar value of its listed companies' securities. As of October 2008, the combined capitalization of all domestic _____ listed companies was US$10.1 trillion.

a. 130-30 fund
b. 1921 recession
c. New York Stock Exchange
d. 100-year flood

31. A _____ is a corporation or mutual organization which provides trading facilities for stock brokers and traders, to trade stocks and other securities. It may be a physical trading room where the traders gather, or a formalised communications network. Creation of a _____ is a strategy of economic development.

a. Primary shares
b. 100-year flood
c. Stock Exchange
d. SEAQ

32. In economics, an _____ is any good (e.g. a commodity) or service brought into one country from another country in a legitimate fashion, typically for use in trade. It is a good that is brought in from another country for sale. _____ goods or services are provided to domestic consumers by foreign producers. An _____ in the receiving country is an export to the sending country.

a. Economic integration
b. Import
c. Incoterms
d. Import quota

33. A _____ is a duty imposed on goods when they are moved across a political boundary. They are usually associated with protectionism, the economic policy of restraining trade between nations. For political reasons, _____s are usually imposed on imported goods, although they may also be imposed on exported goods.

a. 130-30 fund
b. 1921 recession
c. 100-year flood
d. Tariff

34. In economics, _____ is the process by which a firm determines the price and output level that returns the greatest profit. There are several approaches to this problem. The total revenue--total cost method relies on the fact that profit equals revenue minus cost, and the marginal revenue--marginal cost method is based on the fact that total profit in a perfectly competitive market reaches its maximum point where marginal revenue equals marginal cost.

a. Profit margin
b. 100-year flood
c. Profit maximization
d. Normal profit

Chapter 9. Oligopoly and Firm Architecture

1. A true _____ is a specific type of oligopoly where only two producers exist in one market. In reality, this definition is generally used where only two firms have dominant control over a market. In the field of industrial organization, it is the most commonly studied form of oligopoly due to its simplicity.
   a. 100-year flood
   b. 130-30 fund
   c. Megacorpstate
   d. Duopoly

2. The _____ is a measure of the size of firms in relation to the industry and an indicator of the amount of competition among them. Named after economists Orris C. Herfindahl and Albert O. Hirschman, it is an economic concept, widely applied in competition law, antitrust and also technology management. It is defined as the sum of the squares of the market shares of the 50 largest firms within the industry, where the market shares are expressed as percentages.
   a. Vector autoregression
   b. Herfindahl index
   c. Reduced form
   d. Panel data

3. An _____ is a market form in which a market or industry is dominated by a small number of sellers (oligopolists.) Because there are few participants in this type of market, each oligopolist is aware of the actions of the others. The decisions of one firm influence, and are influenced by, the decisions of other firms.
   a. ACEA agreement
   b. Oligopsony
   c. Oligopoly
   d. ACCRA Cost of Living Index

4. In economics, the _____ of an industry is used as an indicator of the relative size of firms in relation to the industry as a whole. It is calculated as the sum of the percent market share of the top n industries. This may also assist in determining the market structure of the industry.
   a. Pacman conjecture
   b. Monopolization
   c. Quasi-rent
   d. Concentration ratio

5. A limit price is the price set by a monopolist to discourage economic entry into a market, and is illegal in many countries. The limit price is the price that the entrant would face upon entering as long as the incumbent firm did not decrease output. The limit price is often lower than the average cost of production or just low enough to make entering not profitable. The quantity produced by the incumbent firm to act as a deterrent to entry is usually larger than would be optimal for a monopolist, but might still produce higher economic profits than would be earned under perfect competition. The problem with _____ as strategic behavior is that once the entrant has entered the market, the quantity used as a threat to deter entry is no longer the incumbent firm's best response.
   a. Limit pricing
   b. Third line forcing
   c. Predatory pricing
   d. Conscious parallelism

6. _____ is one of the four Ps of the marketing mix. The other three aspects are product, promotion, and place. It is also a key variable in microeconomic price allocation theory.
   a. Point of total assumption
   b. Pricing
   c. Guaranteed Maximum Price
   d. Premium pricing

7. A _____ is an expression that compares quantities relative to each other. The most common examples involve two quantities, but any number of quantities can be compared. _____s are represented mathematically by separating each quantity with a colon, for example the _____ 2:3, which is read as the _____ 'two to three'.
   a. 100-year flood
   b. 130-30 fund
   c. Y-intercept
   d. Ratio

Chapter 9. Oligopoly and Firm Architecture

8. In economics, a _____ is a market served by only one firm, but with mandated 'competitive' pricing, so as to second the monopoly held by said firm on said market. Its fundamental feature is low barriers to entry and exit; a perfectly _____ would have no barriers to entry or exit. _____s are characteristed by 'hit and run' entry.
   a. Horizontal market
   b. Contestable market
   c. Perfect market
   d. Market mechanism

9. _____ is an economic model used to describe an industry structure in which companies compete on the amount of output they will produce, which they decide on independently of each other and at the same time. It is named after Antoine Augustin Cournot (1801-1877) after he observed competition in a spring water duopoly. It has the following features:

   - There is more than one firm and all firms produce a homogeneous product, i.e. there is no product differentiation;
   - Firms do not cooperate, i.e. there is no collusion;
   - Firms have market power, i.e. each firm's output decision affects the good's price;
   - The number of firms is fixed;
   - Firms compete in quantities, and choose quantities simultaneously;
   - The firms are economically rational and act strategically, usually seeking to maximize profit given their competitors' decisions.

   An essential assumption of this model is that each firm aims to maximize profits, based on the expectation that its own output decision will not have an effect on the decisions of its rivals. Price is a commonly known decreasing function of total output.

   a. Cournot competition
   b. 130-30 fund
   c. 1921 recession
   d. 100-year flood

10. The _____ curve theory is an economic theory regarding oligopoly and monopolistic competition. When it was created, the idea fundamentally challenged classical economic tenets such as efficient markets and rapidly-changing prices, ideas that underly basic supply and demand models. _____ was an initial attempt to explain sticky prices.
    a. Kinked demand
    b. Precautionary demand
    c. Marginal demand
    d. Kinked demand curve

11. The _____ theory is an economic theory regarding oligopoly and monopolistic competition. When it was created, the idea fundamentally challenged classical economic tenets such as efficient markets and rapidly-changing prices, ideas that underly basic supply and demand models. Kinked demand was an initial attempt to explain sticky prices.
    a. Kinked demand
    b. Precautionary demand
    c. Kinked demand curve
    d. Hicksian demand function

12. Economics:

- _____, the desire to own something and the ability to pay for it
- _____ curve, a graphic representation of a _____ schedule
- _____ deposit, the money in checking accounts
- _____ pull theory, the theory that inflation occurs when _____ for goods and services exceeds existing supplies
- _____ schedule, a table that lists the quantity of a good a person will buy it each different price
- _____ side economics, the school of economics at believes government spending and tax cuts open economy by raising _____

a. McKesson ' Robbins scandal
b. Variability
c. Production
d. Demand

13. In economics, the _____ can be defined as the graph depicting the relationship between the price of a certain commodity, and the amount of it that consumers are willing and able to purchase at that given price. It is a graphic representation of a demand schedule. The _____ for all consumers together follows from the _____ of every individual consumer: the individual demands at each price are added together.
   a. Wage curve
   b. Demand curve
   c. Cost curve
   d. Kuznets curve

14. A _____ is a counterfeit agreement among industries. It is an informal organization of producers that agree to coordinate prices and production. _____s usually occur in an oligopolistic industry, where there is a small number of sellers and usually involve homogeneous products.
   a. 100-year flood
   b. Shanzhai
   c. Shill
   d. Cartel

15. _____ is the transition of a national economy from monopoly control by groups of large businesses to a free market economy. This change rarely arises naturally, and is generally the result of regulation by a governing body.

A modern example of _____ is the economic restructuring of Germany after the fall of the Third Reich in 1945.

   a. Complementary monopoly
   b. Market power
   c. Monopolization
   d. Decartelization

16. _____ is an agreement, usually secretive, which occurs between two or more persons to deceive, mislead or to obtain an objective forbidden by law typically involving fraud or gaining an unfair advantage. It is an agreement among firms to divide the market, set prices kickbacks, or misrepresenting the independence of the relationship between the colluding parties.' All acts effected by _____ are considered void.
   a. Collusion
   b. Bid rigging
   c. Net Book Agreement
   d. Dividing territories

Chapter 9. Oligopoly and Firm Architecture

17. _____ in economics and business is the result of an exchange and from that trade we assign a numerical monetary value to a good, service or asset. If Alice trades Bob 4 apples for an orange, the _____ of an orange is 4 apples. Inversely, the _____ of an apple is 1/4 oranges.
   a. Premium pricing
   b. Price book
   c. Price war
   d. Price

18. The U.S. _____ (EEOC) is a federal agency whose goal is ending employment discrimination. The _____ investigates discrimination complaints based on an individual's race, color, national origin, religion, sex, age, disability and retaliation for reporting and/or opposing a discriminatory practice. The Commission is also tasked with filing suits on behalf of alleged victim(s) of discrimination against employers and as an adjudicatory for claims of discrimination brought against federal agencies.
   a. AD-IA Model
   b. ACEA agreement
   c. ACCRA Cost of Living Index
   d. EEOC

19. The _____ consists of a number of economic theories which describe the nature of the firm, company including its existence, its behaviour, and its relationship with the market.

In simplified terms, the _____ aims to answer these questions:

   1. Existence - why do firms emerge, why are not all transactions in the economy mediated over the market?
   2. Boundaries - why the boundary between firms and the market is located exactly there? Which transactions are performed internally and which are negotiated on the market?
   3. Organization - why are firms structured in such specific way? What is the interplay of formal and informal relationships?

Despite looking simple, these questions are not answered by the established economic theory, which usually views firms as given, and treats them as black boxes without any internal structure.

The First World War period saw a change of emphasis in economic theory away from industry-level analysis which mainly included analysing markets to analysis at the level of the firm, as it became increasingly clear that perfect competition was no longer an adequate model of how firms behaved. Economic theory till then had focussed on trying to understand markets alone and there had been little study on understanding why firms or organisations exist.

   a. Technology gap
   b. Theory of the firm
   c. Policy Ineffectiveness Proposition
   d. Khazzoom-Brookes postulate

20. _____ is the activity of estimating the quantity of a product or service that consumers will purchase. _____ involves techniques including both informal methods, such as educated guesses, and quantitative methods, such as the use of historical sales data or current data from test markets. _____ may be used in making pricing decisions, in assessing future capacity requirements, or in making decisions on whether to enter a new market.
   a. Cost price
   b. Demand forecasting
   c. Finance designations
   d. Financial Reporting

21. _____ is the process of estimation in unknown situations. Prediction is a similar, but more general term. Both can refer to estimation of time series, cross-sectional or longitudinal data.

Chapter 9. Oligopoly and Firm Architecture

a. 130-30 fund
b. 1921 recession
c. 100-year flood
d. Forecasting

22. _____ in its literal sense is the process of transformation of local or regional phenomena into global ones. It can be described as a process by which the people of the world are unified into a single society and function together.

This process is a combination of economic, technological, sociocultural and political forces.

a. Globalization
b. Global Cosmopolitanism
c. Helsinki Process on Globalisation and Democracy
d. Globally Integrated Enterprise

23. _____ Group is one of the largest corporate conglomerates (Keiretsu) in Japan and one of the largest publicly traded companies in the world. Surugacho (Suruga Street) (1856), from One Hundred Famous Views of Edo, by Hiroshige, depicting the Echigoya kimono and money exchange store with Mount Fuji in background. Currently, the _____ Main Building (ä‚‰ä°•æœ¬é¤¨), which houses Sumitomo _____ Banking Corporation, _____ Fudosan, The Chuo _____ Trust and Banking Co.

a. 130-30 fund
b. 1921 recession
c. Mitsui
d. 100-year flood

24. The phrase _____ refers to the aspect of corporate strategy, corporate finance and management dealing with the buying, selling and combining of different companies that can aid, finance, or help a growing company in a given industry grow rapidly without having to create another business entity.

An acquisition, also known as a takeover or a buyout, is the buying of one company (the 'target') by another. An acquisition may be friendly or hostile.

a. Mergers and acquisitions
b. Peace dividend
c. Productive and unproductive labour
d. Political economy

25. The phrase _____ and acquisitions refers to the aspect of corporate strategy, corporate finance and management dealing with the buying, selling and combining of different companies that can aid, finance, or help a growing company in a given industry grow rapidly without having to create another business entity.

An acquisition, also known as a takeover or a buyout, is the buying of one company (the 'target') by another. An acquisition may be friendly or hostile.

a. Differential accumulation
b. Peace dividend
c. Political economy
d. Mergers

26. _____ is a broad label that refers to any individuals or households that use goods and services generated within the economy. The concept of a _____ is used in different contexts, so that the usage and significance of the term may vary.

Typically when business people and economists talk of _____s they are talking about person as _____, an aggregated commodity item with little individuality other than that expressed in the buy/not-buy decision.

Chapter 9. Oligopoly and Firm Architecture

a. 1921 recession
b. 130-30 fund
c. 100-year flood
d. Consumer

27. _____ is subcontracting a process, such as product design or manufacturing, to a third-party company. The decision to outsource is often made in the interest of lowering cost or making better use of time and energy costs, redirecting or conserving energy directed at the competencies of a particular business, or to make more efficient use of land, labor, capital, (information) technology and resources. _____ became part of the business lexicon during the 1980s.

a. Averch-Johnson effect
b. Outsourcing
c. Electronic business
d. Additional Funds Needed

28. In statistics, _____ is a collection of statistical models, and their associated procedures, in which the observed variance is partitioned into components due to different explanatory variables. In its simplest form ANOVA gives a statistical test of whether the means of several groups are all equal, and therefore generalizes Student's two-sample t-test to more than two groups.

There are three conceptual classes of such models:

1. Fixed-effects models assumes that the data came from normal populations which may differ only in their means. (Model 1)
2. Random effects models assume that the data describe a hierarchy of different populations whose differences are constrained by the hierarchy. (Model 2)
3. Mixed-effect models describe situations where both fixed and random effects are present. (Model 3)

In practice, there are several types of ANOVA depending on the number of treatments and the way they are applied to the subjects in the experiment:

- One-way ANOVA is used to test for differences among two or more independent groups. Typically, however, the one-way ANOVA is used to test for differences among at least three groups, since the two-group case can be covered by a T-test (Gossett, 1908.)

a. Analysis of variance
b. ACEA agreement
c. ACCRA Cost of Living Index
d. AD-IA Model

29. In statistics, _____ has two related meanings:

- the arithmetic _____
- the expected value of a random variable, which is also called the population _____.

It is sometimes stated that the '_____' _____s average. This is incorrect if '_____' is taken in the specific sense of 'arithmetic _____' as there are different types of averages: the _____, median, and mode. Other simple statistical analyses use measures of spread, such as range, interquartile range, or standard deviation. For a real-valued random variable X, the _____ is the expectation of X. Note that not every probability distribution has a defined _____ (or variance); see the Cauchy distribution for an example.

Chapter 9. Oligopoly and Firm Architecture

a. 130-30 fund
b. 1921 recession
c. Mean
d. 100-year flood

30. _____ is a comparative concept of the ability and performance of a firm, sub-sector or country to sell and supply goods and/or services in a given market. Although widely used in economics and business management, the usefulness of the concept, particularly in the context of national _____, is vigorously disputed by economists, such as Paul Krugman .

The term may also be applied to markets, where it is used to refer to the extent to which the market structure may be regarded as perfectly competitive.

a. Debt moratorium
b. Competitiveness
c. Countervailing duties
d. Quota share

31. _____ is the removal or simplification of government rules and regulations that constrain the operation of market forces. _____ does not mean elimination of laws against fraud, but eliminating or reducing government control of how business is done, thereby moving toward a more free market.

The stated rationale for '_____' is often that fewer and simpler regulations will lead to a raised level of competitiveness, therefore higher productivity, more efficiency and lower prices overall.

a. Fundamental psychological law
b. Secular basis
c. Macroeconomic policy instruments
d. Deregulation

32. The _____, a unit of the United States Department of Labor, is the principal fact-finding agency for the U.S. government in the broad field of labor economics and statistics. The BLS is an independent national statistical agency that collects, processes, analyzes, and disseminates essential statistical data to the American public, the U.S. Congress, other Federal agencies, State and local governments, business, and labor representatives. The BLS also serves as a statistical resource to the Department of Labor.

a. Gross Regional Product
b. Gross world product
c. Bureau of Labor Statistics
d. Gross national product

33. _____ AG is an international Universal bank with its headquarters in Frankfurt, Germany. The bank employs more than 81,000 people in 76 countries, and has a large presence in Europe, the Americas, Asia Pacific and the emerging markets.

_____ has offices in major financial centers, such as London, Moscow, New York, São Paulo, Singapore, Sydney, Hong Kong and Tokyo.

a. Deutsche Bank
b. Chinese correction
c. Federal Deposit Insurance Corporation
d. Paris Club

34. The Organization of the Petroleum Exporting Countries is a cartel of twelve countries made up of Algeria, Angola, Ecuador, Iran, Iraq, Kuwait, Libya, Nigeria, Qatar, Saudi Arabia, the United Arab Emirates, and Venezuela. The cartel has maintained its headquarters in Vienna since 1965, and hosts regular meetings among the oil ministers of its Member Countries. Indonesia withdrew its membership in _____ in 2008 after it became a net importer of oil, but stated it would likely return if it became a net exporter in the world.

a. ACEA agreement
c. ACCRA Cost of Living Index
b. AD-IA Model
d. OPEC

35. Procter is a surname, and may also refer to:

- Bryan Waller Procter (pseud. Barry Cornwall), English poet
- Goodwin Procter, American law firm
- _____, consumer products multinational

a. Bucket shop
c. Tightness
b. Drawdown
d. Procter ' Gamble

36. A _____ is a public market for the trading of company stock and derivatives at an agreed price; these are securities listed on a stock exchange as well as those only traded privately.

The size of the world _____ was estimated at about $36.6 trillion US at the beginning of October 2008 . The total world derivatives market has been estimated at about $791 trillion face or nominal value, 11 times the size of the entire world economy.

a. Adolph Fischer
c. Adolf Hitler
b. Adam Smith
d. Stock market

Chapter 10. Game Theory and Strategic Behavior

1. _____ is a branch of applied mathematics that is used in the social sciences (most notably economics), biology, engineering, political science, international relations, computer science, and philosophy. _____ attempts to mathematically capture behavior in strategic situations, in which an individual's success in making choices depends on the choices of others. While initially developed to analyze competitions in which one individual does better at another's expense (zero sum games), it has been expanded to treat a wide class of interactions, which are classified according to several criteria.

   a. Discriminatory price auction   b. Proper equilibrium
   c. Game theory   d. Dollar auction

2. The _____ is a trilateral trade bloc in North America created by the governments of the United States, Canada, and Mexico. The agreement creating the trade bloc came into force on January 1, 1994. It superseded the Canada-United States Free Trade Agreement between the U.S. and Canada.

   a. Federal Reserve Bank Notes   b. Case-Shiller Home Price Indices
   c. Demand-side technologies   d. North American Free Trade Agreement

3. In game theory, _____ is a solution concept of a game involving two or more players, in which each player is assumed to know the equilibrium strategies of the other players, and no player has anything to gain by changing only his or her own strategy unilaterally. If each player has chosen a strategy and no player can benefit by changing his or her strategy while the other players keep theirs unchanged, then the current set of strategy choices and the corresponding payoffs constitute a _____.

Stated simply, Amy and Bill are in _____ if Amy is making the best decision she can, taking into account Bill's decision, and Bill is making the best decision he can, taking into account Amy's decision.

   a. Proper equilibrium   b. Lump of labour
   c. Linear production game   d. Nash equilibrium

4. _____ is the removal or simplification of government rules and regulations that constrain the operation of market forces. _____ does not mean elimination of laws against fraud, but eliminating or reducing government control of how business is done, thereby moving toward a more free market.

The stated rationale for '_____' is often that fewer and simpler regulations will lead to a raised level of competitiveness, therefore higher productivity, more efficiency and lower prices overall.

   a. Secular basis   b. Fundamental psychological law
   c. Macroeconomic policy instruments   d. Deregulation

5. _____ in economics and business is the result of an exchange and from that trade we assign a numerical monetary value to a good, service or asset. If Alice trades Bob 4 apples for an orange, the _____ of an orange is 4 apples. Inversely, the _____ of an apple is 1/4 oranges.

   a. Price book   b. Price war
   c. Premium pricing   d. Price

6. A _____ is a counterfeit agreement among industries. It is an informal organization of producers that agree to coordinate prices and production. _____s usually occur in an oligopolistic industry, where there is a small number of sellers and usually involve homogeneous products.

Chapter 10. Game Theory and Strategic Behavior

a. Shill
b. Shanzhai
c. 100-year flood
d. Cartel

7. _____ is the transition of a national economy from monopoly control by groups of large businesses to a free market economy. This change rarely arises naturally, and is generally the result of regulation by a governing body.

A modern example of _____ is the economic restructuring of Germany after the fall of the Third Reich in 1945.

a. Market power
b. Decartelization
c. Complementary monopoly
d. Monopolization

8. In game theory, a _____ is an extensive form game which consists in some number of repetitions of some base game (called a stage game.) The stage game is usually one of the well-studied 2-person games. It captures the idea that a player will have to take into account the impact of his current action on the future actions of other players; this is sometimes called his reputation.

a. Quasi-perfect equilibrium
b. Correlated equilibrium
c. Pursuit-evasion
d. Repeated game

9. _____ refers to the objective and subjective components of the believability of a source or message.

Traditionally, _____ has two key components: trustworthiness and expertise, which both have objective and subjective components. Trustworthiness is a based more on subjective factors, but can include objective measurements such as established reliability.

a. 100-year flood
b. 130-30 fund
c. 1921 recession
d. Credibility

10. _____ is a comparative concept of the ability and performance of a firm, sub-sector or country to sell and supply goods and/or services in a given market. Although widely used in economics and business management, the usefulness of the concept, particularly in the context of national _____, is vigorously disputed by economists, such as Paul Krugman .

The term may also be applied to markets, where it is used to refer to the extent to which the market structure may be regarded as perfectly competitive.

a. Competitiveness
b. Quota share
c. Countervailing duties
d. Debt moratorium

11. _____ is the advantage gained by the initial occupant of a market segment. This advantage may stem from the fact that the first entrant can gain control of resources that followers may not be able to match. Sometimes the first mover is not able to capitalise on its advantage, leaving the opportunity for another firm to gain second-mover advantage.

a. First-mover advantage
b. Continuous Improvement Process
c. Business engineering
d. Cross-docking

12. _____ refers to a company ceasing its operations following its inability to make a profit or to bring in enough revenue to cover its expenses.

Some businesses fail early on. This can occur as a result of poor management skills, insufficient marketing, inability to compete with other similar businesses, or a lack of interest from the public in the business's offerings.

a. Business process automation
b. Business failure
c. Small business
d. Golden Boot Compensation

13. In game theory, a _____ is a game where one player chooses his action before the others choose theirs. Importantly, the later players must have some information of the first's choice, otherwise the difference in time would have no strategic effect. Extensive form representations are usually used for _____s, since they explicitly illustrate the sequential aspects of a game.

a. Sequential game
b. Conglomerate merger
c. Normative economics
d. Comparative economic systems

14. _____ is the process of reasoning backwards in time, from the end of a problem or situation, to determine a sequence of optimal actions. It proceeds by first considering the last time a decision might be made and choosing what to do in any situation at that time. Using this information, one can then determine what to do at the second-to-last time of decision.

a. 100-year flood
b. 1921 recession
c. 130-30 fund
d. Backward induction

15. The _____, a unit of the United States Department of Labor, is the principal fact-finding agency for the U.S. government in the broad field of labor economics and statistics. The BLS is an independent national statistical agency that collects, processes, analyzes, and disseminates essential statistical data to the American public, the U.S. Congress, other Federal agencies, State and local governments, business, and labor representatives. The BLS also serves as a statistical resource to the Department of Labor.

a. Gross national product
b. Bureau of Labor Statistics
c. Gross Regional Product
d. Gross world product

Chapter 11. Pricing Practices

1. _____ is one of the four Ps of the marketing mix. The other three aspects are product, promotion, and place. It is also a key variable in microeconomic price allocation theory.
   a. Guaranteed Maximum Price
   b. Pricing
   c. Point of total assumption
   d. Premium pricing

2. Economics:

   - _____,the desire to own something and the ability to pay for it
   - _____ curve,a graphic representation of a _____ schedule
   - _____ deposit, the money in checking accounts
   - _____ pull theory,the theory that inflation occurs when _____ for goods and services exceeds existing supplies
   - _____ schedule,a table that lists the quantity of a good a person will buy it each different price
   - _____ side economics,the school of economics at believes government spending and tax cuts open economy by raising _____

   a. McKesson ' Robbins scandal
   b. Variability
   c. Demand
   d. Production

3. _____ is a concept in economics which refers to the extent to which an enterprise or a nation actually uses its installed productive capacity. Thus, it refers to the relationship between actual output that 'is' produced with the installed equipment and the potential output which 'could' be produced with it, if capacity was fully used.

   If market demand grows, _____ will rise.

   a. Diseconomies of scale
   b. Marginal product of labor
   c. Capacity utilization
   d. Long-run

4. A _____ or leader is a product sold at a low price (at cost or below cost) to stimulate other, profitable sales. It is a kind of sales promotion, in other words marketing concentrating on a pricing strategy. The price can even be so low that the product is sold at a loss.
   a. Factor price equalization
   b. Two-part tariff
   c. Price ceiling
   d. Loss leader

5. _____ in economics and business is the result of an exchange and from that trade we assign a numerical monetary value to a good, service or asset. If Alice trades Bob 4 apples for an orange, the _____ of an orange is 4 apples. Inversely, the _____ of an apple is 1/4 oranges.
   a. Price war
   b. Premium pricing
   c. Price
   d. Price book

6. _____ exists when sales of identical goods or services are transacted at different prices from the same provider. In a theoretical market with perfect information, no transaction costs or prohibition on secondary exchange (or re-selling) to prevent arbitrage, _____ can only be a feature of monopoly and oligopoly markets, where market power can be exercised. Otherwise, the moment the seller tries to sell the same good at different prices, the buyer at the lower price can arbitrage by selling to the consumer buying at the higher price but with a tiny discount.

a. Price discrimination
b. Lerner Index
c. Transfer pricing
d. Loss leader

7. The _____ consists of a number of economic theories which describe the nature of the firm, company including its existence, its behaviour, and its relationship with the market.

In simplified terms, the _____ aims to answer these questions:

1. Existence - why do firms emerge, why are not all transactions in the economy mediated over the market?
2. Boundaries - why the boundary between firms and the market is located exactly there? Which transactions are performed internally and which are negotiated on the market?
3. Organization - why are firms structured in such specific way? What is the interplay of formal and informal relationships?

Despite looking simple, these questions are not answered by the established economic theory, which usually views firms as given, and treats them as black boxes without any internal structure.

The First World War period saw a change of emphasis in economic theory away from industry-level analysis which mainly included analysing markets to analysis at the level of the firm, as it became increasingly clear that perfect competition was no longer an adequate model of how firms behaved. Economic theory till then had focussed on trying to understand markets alone and there had been little study on understanding why firms or organisations exist.

a. Policy Ineffectiveness Proposition
b. Khazzoom-Brookes postulate
c. Technology gap
d. Theory of the firm

8. A _____ is a duty imposed on goods when they are moved across a political boundary. They are usually associated with protectionism, the economic policy of restraining trade between nations. For political reasons, _____s are usually imposed on imported goods, although they may also be imposed on exported goods.
a. Tariff
b. 100-year flood
c. 1921 recession
d. 130-30 fund

9. _____ refers to the pricing of contributions (assets, tangible and intangible, services, and funds) transferred within an organization. For example, goods from the production division may be sold to the marketing division, or goods from a parent company may be sold to a foreign subsidiary. Since the prices are set within an organization (i.e. controlled), the typical market mechanisms that establish prices for such transactions between third parties may not apply.
a. San Francisco congestion pricing
b. Two-part tariff
c. Rational pricing
d. Transfer pricing

10. _____ describes a deliberate attempt to interfere with the free and fair operation of the market and create artificial, false or misleading appearances with respect to the price of a security, commodity or currency. _____ is prohibited under Section 9(a)(2) of the Securities Exchange Act of 1934, and in Australia under Section s 1041A of the Corporations Act 2001. The Act defines _____ as transactions which create an artificial price or maintain an artificial price for a tradable security.

a. Market manipulation
c. Legal monopoly
b. Net domestic product
d. Managerial economics

11. In neoclassical economics and microeconomics, _____ describes the perfect being a market in which there are many small firms, all producing homogeneous goods. In the short term, such markets are productively inefficient as output will not occur where mc is equal to ac, but allocatively efficient, as output under _____ will always occur where mc is equal to mr, and therefore where mc equals ar. However, in the long term, such markets are both allocatively and productively efficient.

a. General equilibrium
c. Perfect competition
b. Co-operative economics
d. Law of supply

12. In economic theory, _____ is the competitive situation in any market where the conditions necessary for perfect competition are not satisfied. It is a market structure that does not meet the conditions of perfect competition.

Forms of _____ include:

- Monopoly, in which there is only one seller of a good.
- Oligopoly, in which there is a small number of sellers.
- Monopolistic competition, in which there are many sellers producing highly differentiated goods.
- Monopsony, in which there is only one buyer of a good.
- Oligopsony, in which there is a small number of buyers.

There may also be _____ in markets due to buyers or sellers lacking information about prices and the goods being traded.

There may also be _____ due to a time lag in a market.

a. AD-IA Model
c. ACCRA Cost of Living Index
b. ACEA agreement
d. Imperfect competition

13. A _____ or transnational corporation is a corporation or enterprise that manages production or delivers services in more than one country. It can also be referred to as an international corporation.

The first modern MNC is generally thought to be the Dutch East India Company, established in 1602.

a. Rakon
c. Luxembourg Income Study
b. Foreign direct investment
d. Multinational corporation

14. An _____ is an agreement between a taxpayer and a taxing authority on an appropriate transfer pricing methodology (TPM) for some set of transactions at issue (called 'Covered Transactions'.)

Most _____s involve US taxpayers and the US Internal Revenue Service (IRS), but _____s are also made outside the United States.

Bilateral and multilateral _____ sAdvance Pricing Agreements are generally bi- or multilateral--i.e., they also include agreements between the taxpayer and one or more foreign tax administrations under the authority of the mutual agreement procedure (MAP) specified in income tax treaties.

- a. Offshore banking
- c. Offshore bank
- b. ACCRA Cost of Living Index
- d. Advance pricing agreement

15. _____ is a pricing method used by companies. It is used primarily because it is easy to calculate and requires little information. There are several varieties, but the common thread in all of them is that one first calculates the cost of the product, then includes an additional amount to represent profit.

- a. Cost-plus pricing
- c. Rational pricing
- b. Best available rate
- d. Target costing

16. _____, net margin, net _____ or net profit ratio all refer to a measure of profitability. It is calculated by finding the net profit as a percentage of the revenue.

$$\text{Net profit margin} = \frac{\text{Net profit (after taxes)}}{\text{Revenue}} \times 100$$

The _____ is mostly used for internal comparison.

- a. 100-year flood
- c. Profit maximization
- b. Normal profit
- d. Profit margin

17. In economics, _____ is equal to total cost divided by the number of goods produced (the output quantity, Q.) It is also equal to the sum of average variable costs (total variable costs divided by Q) plus average fixed costs (total fixed costs divided by Q.) _____ s may be dependent on the time period considered (increasing production may be expensive or impossible in the short term, for example.)

- a. Explicit cost
- c. Average cost
- b. Average fixed cost
- d. Average variable cost

18. _____ is a pricing technique applied to public goods, which is a particular case of a Lindahl equilibrium. Instead of different demands for the same public good, we consider the demands for a public good in different periods of the day, month or year, then finding the optimal capacity (quantity supplied) and, afterwards, the optimal peak-load prices.

This has particular applications in public goods such as public urban transportation, where day demand (peak period) is usually much higher than night demand (off-peak period.)

- a. Fiscal imbalance
- c. Peak-load pricing
- b. Cobra effect
- d. Demand management

19. A _____ is a price discrimination technique in which the price of a product or service is composed of two parts - a lump-sum fee as well as a per-unit charge. In general, price discrimination techniques only occur in partially or fully monopolistic markets. It is designed to enable the firm to capture more consumer surplus than it otherwise would in a non-discriminating pricing environment.

Chapter 11. Pricing Practices

a. Penetration pricing
c. Price floor
b. Two-part tariff
d. Big ticket item

20. The _____ is an important selective, mainly private, international organization designed by its founders to supervise and liberalize international trade. The organization officially commenced on 1 January 1995, under the Marrakesh Agreement, succeeding the 1947 General Agreement on Tariffs and Trade (GATT.)

The _____ deals with regulation of trade between participating countries; it provides a framework for negotiating and formalising trade agreements, and a dispute resolution process aimed at enforcing participants' adherence to _____ agreements which are signed by representatives of member governments and ratified by their parliaments.

a. 2009 G-20 London summit protests
b. Backus-Kehoe-Kydland consumption correlation puzzle
c. Bio-energy village
d. World Trade Organization

21. _____ is the a method of technical and economic research of the systems for purpose to optimize a parity between system's consumer functions or properties and expenses to achieve those functions or properties.

This methodology for continuous perfection of production, industrial technologies, organizational structures was developed by Juryj Sobolev in 1948 at the 'Perm telephone factory'

- 1948 Juryj Sobolev - the first success in application of a method analysis at the 'Perm telephone factory'.
- 1949 - the first application for the invention as result of use of the new method.

Today in economically developed countries practically each enterprise or the company use methodology of the kind of functional-cost analysis as a practice of the quality management, most full satisfying to principles of standards of series ISO 9000.

- Interest of consumer not in products itself, but the advantage which it will receive from its usage.
- The consumer aspires to reduce his expenses
- Functions needed by consumer can be executed in the various ways, and, hence, with various efficiency and expenses. Among possible alternatives of realization of functions exist such in which the parity of quality and the price is the optimal for the consumer.

The goal of _____ is achievement of the highest consumer satisfaction of production at simultaneous decrease in all kinds of industrial expenses Classical _____ has three English synonyms - Value Engineering, Value Management, Value Analysis.

a. Monopoly wage
c. Function cost analysis
b. Willingness to pay
d. Staple financing

22. A _____ is a public market for the trading of company stock and derivatives at an agreed price; these are securities listed on a stock exchange as well as those only traded privately.

The size of the world _____ was estimated at about $36.6 trillion US at the beginning of October 2008. The total world derivatives market has been estimated at about $791 trillion face or nominal value, 11 times the size of the entire world economy.

a. Adolph Fischer
b. Adolf Hitler
c. Adam Smith
d. Stock market

23. _____ is the process of understanding, anticipating and influencing consumer behavior in order to maximize revenue or profits from a fixed, perishable resource This process was first discovered by Dr. Matt H. Keller. The challenge is to sell the right resources to the right customer at the right time for the right price.

a. Yield management
b. Freebie marketing
c. Coopetition
d. Subscription

24. The _____ is an independent agency of the United States government, established in 1914 by the _____ Act. Its principal mission is the promotion of 'consumer protection' and the elimination and prevention of what regulators perceive to be harmfully 'anti-competitive' business practices, such as coercive monopoly.

The _____ Act was one of President Wilson's major acts against trusts.

a. 130-30 fund
b. Federal Trade Commission
c. 1921 recession
d. 100-year flood

25. The _____ captures an expanded spectrum of values and criteria for measuring organizational (and societal) success: economic, ecological and social. With the ratification of the United Nations and ICLEI _____ standard for urban and community accounting in early 2007, this became the dominant approach to public sector full cost accounting. Similar UN standards apply to natural capital and human capital measurement to assist in measurements required by _____, e.g. the ecoBudget standard for reporting ecological footprint.

a. Missing market
b. Leapfrogging
c. Social welfare function
d. Triple bottom line

26. _____s is the social science that studies the production, distribution, and consumption of goods and services. The term _____s comes from the Ancient Greek οá¼°κονομῖα from οá¼¶κος (oikos, 'house') + vÏŒμος (nomos, 'custom' or 'law'), hence 'rules of the house(hold)'. Current _____ models developed out of the broader field of political economy in the late 19th century, owing to a desire to use an empirical approach more akin to the physical sciences.

a. Economic
b. Inflation
c. Energy economics
d. Opportunity cost

27. _____ is the practice of selling a product or service at a very low price, intending to drive competitors out of the market, or create barriers to entry for potential new competitors. If competitors or potential competitors cannot sustain equal or lower prices without losing money, they go out of business or choose not to enter the business. The predatory merchant then has fewer competitors or is even a de facto monopoly, and can then raise prices above what the market would otherwise bear.

a. Group boycott
b. Third line forcing
c. Restraint of trade
d. Predatory pricing

Chapter 12. Regulation and Antitrust: The Role of Government in the Economy

1. Economics:

   - _____, the desire to own something and the ability to pay for it
   - _____ curve, a graphic representation of a _____ schedule
   - _____ deposit, the money in checking accounts
   - _____ pull theory, the theory that inflation occurs when _____ for goods and services exceeds existing supplies
   - _____ schedule, a table that lists the quantity of a good a person will buy it each different price
   - _____ side economics, the school of economics at believes government spending and tax cuts open economy by raising _____

   a. Variability
   b. Demand
   c. McKesson ' Robbins scandal
   d. Production

2. _____s is the social science that studies the production, distribution, and consumption of goods and services. The term _____s comes from the Ancient Greek οἰκονομία from οἶκος (oikos, 'house') + νόμος (nomos, 'custom' or 'law'), hence 'rules of the house(hold)'. Current _____ models developed out of the broader field of political economy in the late 19th century, owing to a desire to use an empirical approach more akin to the physical sciences.

   a. Opportunity cost
   b. Inflation
   c. Energy economics
   d. Economic

3. In economic theory, _____ is the competitive situation in any market where the conditions necessary for perfect competition are not satisfied. It is a market structure that does not meet the conditions of perfect competition.

   Forms of _____ include:

   - Monopoly, in which there is only one seller of a good.
   - Oligopoly, in which there is a small number of sellers.
   - Monopolistic competition, in which there are many sellers producing highly differentiated goods.
   - Monopsony, in which there is only one buyer of a good.
   - Oligopsony, in which there is a small number of buyers.

   There may also be _____ in markets due to buyers or sellers lacking information about prices and the goods being traded.

   There may also be _____ due to a time lag in a market.

   a. Imperfect competition
   b. ACEA agreement
   c. ACCRA Cost of Living Index
   d. AD-IA Model

4. _____ is a common market structure where many competing producers sell products that are differentiated from one another (ie. the products are substitutes, but are not exactly alike.) Many markets are monopolistically competitive, common examples include the markets for restaurants, cereal, clothing, shoes and service industries in large cities.

   a. Perfect competition
   b. Mathematical economics
   c. Financial crisis
   d. Monopolistic competition

5. In economics, a _____ exists when a specific individual or enterprise has sufficient control over a particular product or service to determine significantly the terms on which other individuals shall have access to it. Monopolies are thus characterized by a lack of economic competition for the good or service that they provide and a lack of viable substitute goods. The verb 'monopolize' refers to the process by which a firm gains persistently greater market share than what is expected under perfect competition.
   a. Monopoly
   b. 130-30 fund
   c. 100-year flood
   d. 1921 recession

6. An _____ is a market form in which a market or industry is dominated by a small number of sellers (oligopolists.) Because there are few participants in this type of market, each oligopolist is aware of the actions of the others. The decisions of one firm influence, and are influenced by, the decisions of other firms.
   a. ACEA agreement
   b. ACCRA Cost of Living Index
   c. Oligopsony
   d. Oligopoly

7. A _____ is a set of exclusive rights granted by a state to an inventor or his assignee for a limited period of time in exchange for a disclosure of an invention.

The procedure for granting _____s, the requirements placed on the _____ee and the extent of the exclusive rights vary widely between countries according to national laws and international agreements. Typically, however, a _____ application must include one or more claims defining the invention which must be new, inventive, and useful or industrially applicable.

   a. Patent
   b. Bona fide occupational qualification
   c. Long service leave
   d. Bank regulation

8. In neoclassical economics and microeconomics, _____ describes the perfect being a market in which there are many small firms, all producing homogeneous goods. In the short term, such markets are productively inefficient as output will not occur where mc is equal to ac, but allocatively efficient, as output under _____ will always occur where mc is equal to mr, and therefore where mc equals ar. However, in the long term, such markets are both allocatively and productively efficient.
   a. Law of supply
   b. Co-operative economics
   c. General equilibrium
   d. Perfect competition

9. _____ is the removal or simplification of government rules and regulations that constrain the operation of market forces. _____ does not mean elimination of laws against fraud, but eliminating or reducing government control of how business is done, thereby moving toward a more free market.

The stated rationale for '_____' is often that fewer and simpler regulations will lead to a raised level of competitiveness, therefore higher productivity, more efficiency and lower prices overall.

   a. Macroeconomic policy instruments
   b. Deregulation
   c. Secular basis
   d. Fundamental psychological law

10. _____ is the practice of influencing decisions made by government. It includes all attempts to influence legislators and officials, whether by other legislators, constituents or organized groups. A lobbyist is a person who tries to influence legislation on behalf of a special interest or a member of a lobby.

Chapter 12. Regulation and Antitrust: The Role of Government in the Economy

a. Adam Smith
b. Adolph Fischer
c. Lobbying
d. Adolf Hitler

11. _____ in economics and business is the result of an exchange and from that trade we assign a numerical monetary value to a good, service or asset. If Alice trades Bob 4 apples for an orange, the _____ of an orange is 4 apples. Inversely, the _____ of an apple is 1/4 oranges.

a. Premium pricing
b. Price book
c. Price war
d. Price

12. _____ is a broad label that refers to any individuals or households that use goods and services generated within the economy. The concept of a _____ is used in different contexts, so that the usage and significance of the term may vary.

Typically when business people and economists talk of _____s they are talking about person as _____, an aggregated commodity item with little individuality other than that expressed in the buy/not-buy decision.

a. 1921 recession
b. 100-year flood
c. Consumer
d. 130-30 fund

13. _____ laws are designed to ensure fair competition and the free flow of truthful information in the marketplace. The laws are designed to prevent businesses that engage in fraud or specified unfair practices from gaining an advantage over competitors and may provide additional protection for the weak and unable to take care of themselves. _____ laws are a form of government regulation which protects the interests of consumers.

a. Global warming
b. Consumer protection
c. Dow Jones Industrial Average
d. History of minimum wage

14. _____ is one of the four Ps of the marketing mix. The other three aspects are product, promotion, and place. It is also a key variable in microeconomic price allocation theory.

a. Premium pricing
b. Point of total assumption
c. Guaranteed Maximum Price
d. Pricing

15. Competition law, known in the United States as _____ law, has three main elements:

- prohibiting agreements or practices that restrict free trading and competition between business entities. This includes in particular the repression of cartels.
- banning abusive behaviour by a firm dominating a market, or anti-competitive practices that tend to lead to such a dominant position. Practices controlled in this way may include predatory pricing, tying, price gouging, refusal to deal, and many others.
- supervising the mergers and acquisitions of large corporations, including some joint ventures. Transactions that are considered to threaten the competitive process can be prohibited altogether, or approved subject to 'remedies' such as an obligation to divest part of the merged business or to offer licences or access to facilities to enable other businesses to continue competing.

78   *Chapter 12. Regulation and Antitrust: The Role of Government in the Economy*

The substance and practice of competition law varies from jurisdiction to jurisdiction. Protecting the interests of consumers (consumer welfare) and ensuring that entrepreneurs have an opportunity to compete in the market economy are often treated as important objectives. Competition law is closely connected with law on deregulation of access to markets, state aids and subsidies, the privatisation of state owned assets and the establishment of independent sector regulators. In recent decades, competition law has been viewed as a way to provide better public services.

- a. Anti-Inflation Act
- b. United Kingdom competition law
- c. Antitrust
- d. Intellectual property law

16. _____, known in the United States as antitrust law, has three main elements:

- prohibiting agreements or practices that restrict free trading and competition between business entities. This includes in particular the repression of cartels.
- banning abusive behaviour by a firm dominating a market, or anti-competitive practices that tend to lead to such a dominant position. Practices controlled in this way may include predatory pricing, tying, price gouging, refusal to deal, and many others.
- supervising the mergers and acquisitions of large corporations, including some joint ventures. Transactions that are considered to threaten the competitive process can be prohibited altogether, or approved subject to 'remedies' such as an obligation to divest part of the merged business or to offer licences or access to facilities to enable other businesses to continue competing.

The substance and practice of _____ varies from jurisdiction to jurisdiction. Protecting the interests of consumers (consumer welfare) and ensuring that entrepreneurs have an opportunity to compete in the market economy are often treated as important objectives. _____ is closely connected with law on deregulation of access to markets, state aids and subsidies, the privatisation of state owned assets and the establishment of independent sector regulators. In recent decades, _____ has been viewed as a way to provide better public services.

- a. Hostile work environment
- b. Fee simple
- c. Due diligence
- d. Competition law

17. A _____ refers to any type debt instrument, such as a loan, bond, mortgage that does not have a fixed rate of interest over the life of the instrument. Such debt typically uses an index or other base rate for establishing the interest rate for each relevant period. One of the most common rates to use as the basis for applying interest rates is the London Inter-bank Offered Rate, or LIBOR
- a. Money market
- b. Moneylender
- c. Disposal tax effect
- d. Floating interest rate

18. The _____ is an independent agency of the United States government, established in 1914 by the _____ Act. Its principal mission is the promotion of 'consumer protection' and the elimination and prevention of what regulators perceive to be harmfully 'anti-competitive' business practices, such as coercive monopoly.

The _____ Act was one of President Wilson's major acts against trusts.

Chapter 12. Regulation and Antitrust: The Role of Government in the Economy

a. 100-year flood
b. 1921 recession
c. Federal Trade Commission
d. 130-30 fund

19. The _____ of 1914 (15 U.S.C §§ 41-58, as amended) established the Federal Trade Commission (FTC), a bipartisan body of five members appointed by the President of the United States for seven year terms. This Commission was authorized to issue Cease and Desist orders to large corporations to curb unfair trade practices. This Act also gave more flexibility to the US congress for judicial matters.

a. Minimum wage law
b. Buydown
c. Competition law theory
d. Federal Trade Commission Act

20. _____ is a cross-disciplinary area concerned with protecting the safety, health and welfare of people engaged in work or employment. As a secondary effect, it may also protect co-workers, family members, employers, customers, suppliers, nearby communities, and other members of the public who are impacted by the workplace environment. It may involve interactions among many subject areas, including occupational medicine, occupational (or industrial) hygiene, public health, safety engineering, chemistry, health physics, ergonomics, toxicology, epidemiology, environmental health, industrial relations, public policy, sociology, and occupational health psychology.

a. ACEA agreement
b. AD-IA Model
c. Occupational Safety and Health
d. ACCRA Cost of Living Index

21. The United States _____ is an agency of the United States Department of Labor. It was created by Congress under the Occupational Safety and Health Act, signed by President Richard M. Nixon, on December 29, 1970. Its mission is to prevent work-related injuries, illnesses, and deaths by issuing and enforcing rules (called standards) for workplace safety and health.

a. ACCRA Cost of Living Index
b. ACEA agreement
c. AD-IA Model
d. Occupational Safety and Health Administration

22. An _____ is quite usually a standard guarantee from the seller of a product that specifies the extent to which the quality or performance of the product is assured and states the conditions under which the product can be returned, replaced, or repaired. It is often given in the form of a specific, written 'Warranty' document. However, a warranty may also arise by operation of law based upon the seller's description of the goods, and perhaps their source and quality, and any material deviation from that specification would violate the guarantee.

a. ACEA agreement
b. ACCRA Cost of Living Index
c. AD-IA Model
d. Express warranty

23. The _____ of 1938 is a United States federal law that amended the Federal Trade Commission Act to add the clause 'unfair or deceptive acts or practices in commerce are hereby declared unlawful' to the Section 5 prohibition of unfair methods of competition, in order to protect consumers as well as competition.

1938 amendment to the federal trade commission act that authorized the FTC to restrict unfair or deceptive acts; also called the advertising act. Until this amendment was passed, the FTC could only restrict practices that were unfair to competitors.

a. Human rights in Brazil
b. Wheeler-Lea Act
c. Merger guidelines
d. Fee simple

Chapter 12. Regulation and Antitrust: The Role of Government in the Economy

24. _____ is a practice of protecting the environment, on individual, organisational or governmental level, for the benefit of the natural environment and (or) humans.

Due to the pressures of population and technology the biophysical environment is being degraded, sometimes permanently. This has been recognised and governments began placing restraints on activities that caused environmental degradation.

   a. AD-IA Model
   b. Environmental Protection
   c. ACEA agreement
   d. ACCRA Cost of Living Index

25. A _____ describes one of a number of pieces of legislation relating to the reduction of smog and air pollution in general. The use by governments to enforce clean air standards has contributed to an improvement in human health and longer life spans. Critics argue it has also sapped corporate profits and contributed to outsourcing, while defenders counter that improved environmental air quality has generated more jobs than it has eliminated.
   a. 130-30 fund
   b. Clean Air Act
   c. Smog
   d. 100-year flood

26. In economics, a _____ exists when the production or use of goods and services by the market is not efficient. That is, there exists another outcome where all involved can be made better off. _____s can be viewed as scenarios where individuals' pursuit of pure self-interest leads to results that are not efficient - that can be improved upon from the societal point-of-view.
   a. Fixed exchange rate
   b. General equilibrium
   c. Financial economics
   d. Market failure

27. The _____ refers to the 'common well-being' or 'general welfare.' The _____ is central to policy debates, politics, democracy and the nature of government itself. While nearly everyone claims that aiding the common well-being or general welfare is positive, there is little, if any, consensus on what exactly constitutes the _____.

There are different views on how many members of the public must benefit from an action before it can be declared to be in the _____: at one extreme, an action has to benefit every single member of society in order to be truly in the _____; at the other extreme, any action can be in the _____ as long as it benefits some of the population and harms none.

   a. Power Elite
   b. Public interest
   c. Stealth tax
   d. Second-class citizen

28. _____ is an economic theory holding that regulation is supplied in response to the demand of the public for the correction of inefficient or inequitable market practices. Regulation is assumed initially to benefit society as a whole rather than particular vested interests. The regulatory body is considered to represent the interest of the society in which it operates rather than the private interests of the regulators.
   a. Paradox of voting
   b. Rational ignorance
   c. Public choice
   d. Public interest theory

29. _____ is a common concept in economics, and gives rise to derived concepts such as consumer debt. Generally _____ is defined by opposition to production. But the precise definition can vary because different schools of economists define production quite differently.

Chapter 12. Regulation and Antitrust: The Role of Government in the Economy

a. Foreclosure data providers
b. Federal Reserve Bank Notes
c. Cash or share options
d. Consumption

30. _____ is a fee paid on borrowed assets. It is the price paid for the use of borrowed money, or, money earned by deposited funds. Assets that are sometimes lent with _____ include money, shares, consumer goods through hire purchase, major assets such as aircraft, and even entire factories in finance lease arrangements.
   a. Insolvency
   b. Interest
   c. Asset protection
   d. Internal debt

31. In microeconomics, _____ is quite simply the conversion of inputs into outputs. It is an economic process that uses resources to create a good or service that is suitable for exchange. This can include manufacturing, storing, shipping, and packaging.
   a. Production
   b. MET
   c. Solved
   d. Red Guards

32. In economics _____ is defined as the sum of private and external costs. Economic theorists ascribe individual decision-making to a calculation costs and benefits. Rational choice theory assumes that individuals only consider their own private costs when making decisions, not the costs that may be borne by others.
   a. Khozraschyot
   b. Cost-Volume-Profit Analysis
   c. Psychic cost
   d. Social cost

33. To _____ is to impose a financial charge or other levy upon a taxpayer by a state or the functional equivalent of a state.

_____es are also imposed by many subnational entities. _____es consist of direct _____ or indirect _____, and may be paid in money or as its labour equivalent (often but not always unpaid.)

   a. 1921 recession
   b. 130-30 fund
   c. 100-year flood
   d. Tax

34. In economics, an _____ or spillover of an economic transaction is an impact on a party that is not directly involved in the transaction. In such a case, prices do not reflect the full costs or benefits in production or consumption of a product or service. A positive impact is called an external benefit, while a negative impact is called an external cost.
   a. Existence value
   b. Environmental tariff
   c. Environmental impact assessment
   d. Externality

35. _____ describes a deliberate attempt to interfere with the free and fair operation of the market and create artificial, false or misleading appearances with respect to the price of a security, commodity or currency. _____ is prohibited under Section 9(a)(2) of the Securities Exchange Act of 1934, and in Australia under Section s 1041A of the Corporations Act 2001. The Act defines _____ as transactions which create an artificial price or maintain an artificial price for a tradable security.
   a. Net domestic product
   b. Legal monopoly
   c. Managerial economics
   d. Market manipulation

36. A _____ is the transfer of wealth from one party (such as a person or company) to another. A _____ is usually made in exchange for the provision of goods, services or both, or to fulfill a legal obligation.

Chapter 12. Regulation and Antitrust: The Role of Government in the Economy

The simplest and oldest form of _____ is barter, the exchange of one good or service for another.

a. Soft count
c. Social gravity

b. Going concern
d. Payment

37. Examples of _____ include:

- A beekeeper keeps the bees for their honey. A side effect or externality associated with his activity is the pollination of surrounding crops by the bees. The value generated by the pollination may be more important than the value of the harvested honey.

- An individual planting an attractive garden in front of his house may provide benefits to others living in the area, and even financial benefits in the form of increased property values for all property owners.

- An individual buying a product that is interconnected in a network (e.g., a video cellphone) will increase the usefulness of such phones to other people who have a video cellphone. When each new user of a product increases the value of the same product owned by others, the phenomenon is called a network externality or a network effect. Network externalities often have 'tipping points' where, suddenly, the product reaches general acceptance and near-universal usage, a phenomenon which can be seen in the near universal take-up of cellphones in some Scandinavian countries.

- Knowledge spillover of inventions and information - once an invention (or most other forms of practical information) is discovered or made more easily accessible, others benefit by exploiting the invention or information. Copyright and intellectual property law are mechanisms to allow the inventor or creator to benefit from a temporary, state-protected monopoly in return for 'sharing' the information through publication or other means.

a. Total Economic Value
c. Weighted average cost of carbon

b. Positive externalities
d. Negative externalities

38. The phrase _____ and acquisitions refers to the aspect of corporate strategy, corporate finance and management dealing with the buying, selling and combining of different companies that can aid, finance, or help a growing company in a given industry grow rapidly without having to create another business entity.

An acquisition, also known as a takeover or a buyout, is the buying of one company (the 'target') by another. An acquisition may be friendly or hostile.

a. Differential accumulation
c. Mergers

b. Political economy
d. Peace dividend

39. A public utility (usually just utility) is an organization that maintains the infrastructure for a public service (often also providing a service using that infrastructure.) _____ are subject to forms of public control and regulation ranging from local community-based groups to state-wide government monopolies. Common arguments in favor of regulation include the desire to control market power, facilitate competition, promote investment or system expansion, or stabilize markets.

Chapter 12. Regulation and Antitrust: The Role of Government in the Economy

a. Public utilities
b. 1921 recession
c. 100-year flood
d. 130-30 fund

40. The _____ is the tendency of companies to engage in excessive amounts of capital accumulation in order to expand the volume of their profits. If companies profits to capital ratio is regulated at a certain percentage then there is a strong incentive for companies to over-invest in order to increase profits overall. This goes against any optimal efficiency point for capital that the company may have calculated as higher profit is almost always desired over and above efficiency.
   a. Additional Funds Needed
   b. Elemental cost planning
   c. Affinity diagram
   d. Averch-Johnson effect

41. In economics, _____ is a measure of the relative satisfaction from consumption of various goods and services. Given this measure, one may speak meaningfully of increasing or decreasing _____, and thereby explain economic behavior in terms of attempts to increase one's _____. For illustrative purposes, changes in _____ are sometimes expressed in units called utils.
   a. Expected utility hypothesis
   b. Utility function
   c. Ordinal utility
   d. Utility

42. _____ in its literal sense is the process of transformation of local or regional phenomena into global ones. It can be described as a process by which the people of the world are unified into a single society and function together.

This process is a combination of economic, technological, sociocultural and political forces.

   a. Globally Integrated Enterprise
   b. Helsinki Process on Globalisation and Democracy
   c. Global Cosmopolitanism
   d. Globalization

43. _____ was a predominant American integrated oil producing, transporting, refining, and marketing company. Established in 1870 as an Ohio Corporation, it was the largest oil refiner in the world and operated as a major company trust and was one of the world's first and largest multinational corporations until it was broken up by the United States Supreme Court in 1911. John D. Rockefeller was a founder, chairman and major shareholder, and the company made him a billionaire and eventually the richest man in history.
   a. Standard Oil
   b. 100-year flood
   c. 1921 recession
   d. 130-30 fund

44. The _____ of 1936 (or Anti-Price Discrimination Act, 15 U.S.C. § 13) is a United States federal law that prohibits what were considered, at the time of passage, to be anticompetitive practices by producers, specifically price discrimination. It grew out of practices in which chain stores were allowed to purchase goods at lower prices than other retailers.
   a. Robinson-Patman Act
   b. Contract theory
   c. Feoffee
   d. Flextime

45. An _____ is an equitable remedy in the form of a court order, whereby a party is required to do certain acts. The party that fails to adhere to the _____ faces civil or criminal penalties and may have to pay damages or accept sanctions for failing to follow the court's order. In some cases, breaches of _____ s are considered serious criminal offences that merit arrest and possible prison sentences.
   a. AD-IA Model
   b. Injunction
   c. ACEA agreement
   d. ACCRA Cost of Living Index

46. The _____ is a measure of the size of firms in relation to the industry and an indicator of the amount of competition among them. Named after economists Orris C. Herfindahl and Albert O. Hirschman, it is an economic concept, widely applied in competition law, antitrust and also technology management. It is defined as the sum of the squares of the market shares of the 50 largest firms within the industry, where the market shares are expressed as percentages.
   a. Reduced form
   b. Herfindahl index
   c. Panel data
   d. Vector autoregression

47. _____ is an agreement, usually secretive, which occurs between two or more persons to deceive, mislead or to obtain an objective forbidden by law typically involving fraud or gaining an unfair advantage. It is an agreement among firms to divide the market, set prices kickbacks, or misrepresenting the independence of the relationship between the colluding parties.' All acts effected by _____ are considered void.
   a. Net Book Agreement
   b. Dividing territories
   c. Bid rigging
   d. Collusion

48. _____ is a term used in competition law to describe price-fixing between competitors in an oligopoly that occurs without an actual spoken agreement between the parties. Instead, one competitor will take the lead in raising prices. The others will then follow suit, raising their prices by the same amount, with the unspoken mutual understanding that all will reap greater profits from the higher prices so long as none attempts to undercut the others.
   a. Social dumping
   b. Group boycott
   c. Net Book Agreement
   d. Conscious parallelism

49. _____ is the practice of selling a product or service at a very low price, intending to drive competitors out of the market, or create barriers to entry for potential new competitors. If competitors or potential competitors cannot sustain equal or lower prices without losing money, they go out of business or choose not to enter the business. The predatory merchant then has fewer competitors or is even a de facto monopoly, and can then raise prices above what the market would otherwise bear.
   a. Restraint of trade
   b. Third line forcing
   c. Predatory pricing
   d. Group boycott

50. _____ exists when sales of identical goods or services are transacted at different prices from the same provider. In a theoretical market with perfect information, no transaction costs or prohibition on secondary exchange (or re-selling) to prevent arbitrage, _____ can only be a feature of monopoly and oligopoly markets, where market power can be exercised. Otherwise, the moment the seller tries to sell the same good at different prices, the buyer at the lower price can arbitrage by selling to the consumer buying at the higher price but with a tiny discount.
   a. Lerner Index
   b. Transfer pricing
   c. Loss leader
   d. Price discrimination

51. The _____ consists of a number of economic theories which describe the nature of the firm, company including its existence, its behaviour, and its relationship with the market.

Chapter 12. Regulation and Antitrust: The Role of Government in the Economy

In simplified terms, the _____ aims to answer these questions:

1. Existence - why do firms emerge, why are not all transactions in the economy mediated over the market?
2. Boundaries - why the boundary between firms and the market is located exactly there? Which transactions are performed internally and which are negotiated on the market?
3. Organization - why are firms structured in such specific way? What is the interplay of formal and informal relationships?

Despite looking simple, these questions are not answered by the established economic theory, which usually views firms as given, and treats them as black boxes without any internal structure.

The First World War period saw a change of emphasis in economic theory away from industry-level analysis which mainly included analysing markets to analysis at the level of the firm, as it became increasingly clear that perfect competition was no longer an adequate model of how firms behaved. Economic theory till then had focussed on trying to understand markets alone and there had been little study on understanding why firms or organisations exist.

a. Policy Ineffectiveness Proposition
b. Technology gap
c. Theory of the firm
d. Khazzoom-Brookes postulate

52. The _____, a United States federal financial statute law passed in 1980, gave the Federal Reserve greater control over non-member banks.

- It forced all banks to abide by the Fed's rules.
- It allowed banks to merge.
- It removed the power of the Federal Reserve Board of Governors under the Glass-Steagall Act and Regulation Q to set the interest rates of savings accounts.
- It raised the deposit insurance of US banks and credit unions from $40,000 to $100,000.
- It allowed credit unions and savings and loans to offer checkable deposits.
- Allowed institutions to charge any interest rates they chose.

a. Cash flow loan
b. Capital guarantee
c. Market-based instruments
d. Depository Institutions Deregulation and Monetary Control Act

53. In economics, an _____ is any good (e.g. a commodity) or service brought into one country from another country in a legitimate fashion, typically for use in trade. It is a good that is brought in from another country for sale. _____ goods or services are provided to domestic consumers by foreign producers. An _____ in the receiving country is an export to the sending country.

a. Economic integration
b. Import
c. Incoterms
d. Import quota

Chapter 12. Regulation and Antitrust: The Role of Government in the Economy

54. A _____ is a duty imposed on goods when they are moved across a political boundary. They are usually associated with protectionism, the economic policy of restraining trade between nations. For political reasons, _____s are usually imposed on imported goods, although they may also be imposed on exported goods.

   a. Tariff
   b. 1921 recession
   c. 100-year flood
   d. 130-30 fund

55. _____ is a form of fraud in which a commercial contract is promised to one party even though for the sake of appearance several other parties also present a bid. This form of collusion is illegal in most countries. It is a form of price fixing and market allocation, often practised where contracts are determined by a call for bids, for example in the case of government construction contracts.

   a. Predatory pricing
   b. Limit pricing
   c. Net Book Agreement
   d. Bid rigging

56. A _____ is a counterfeit agreement among industries. It is an informal organization of producers that agree to coordinate prices and production. _____s usually occur in an oligopolistic industry, where there is a small number of sellers and usually involve homogeneous products.

   a. Shill
   b. Shanzhai
   c. 100-year flood
   d. Cartel

57. _____ is the transition of a national economy from monopoly control by groups of large businesses to a free market economy. This change rarely arises naturally, and is generally the result of regulation by a governing body.

   A modern example of _____ is the economic restructuring of Germany after the fall of the Third Reich in 1945.

   a. Complementary monopoly
   b. Market power
   c. Monopolization
   d. Decartelization

58. An _____ is a type of protectionist trade restriction that sets a physical limit on the quantity of a good that can be imported into a country in a given period of time. Quotas, like other trade restrictions, are used to benefit the producers of a good in a domestic economy at the expense of all consumers of the good in that economy.

   Critics say quotas often lead to corruption (bribes to get a quota allocation), smuggling (circumventing a quota), and higher prices for consumers.

   a. Agreement on Agriculture
   b. International Monetary Systems
   c. Import quota
   d. Economic integration

59. The _____ commenced in September 1986 and continued until April 1994. The round, based on the General Agreement on Tariffs and Trade (GATT) ministerial meeting in Geneva (1982), was launched in Punta del Este in Uruguay (hence the name), followed by negotiations in Montreal, Geneva, Brussels, Washington, D.C., and Tokyo, with the 20 agreements finally being signed in Marrakech - the Marrakesh Agreement. The Round transformed the GATT into the World Trade Organization.

   a. Uruguay round
   b. ACCRA Cost of Living Index
   c. AD-IA Model
   d. ACEA agreement

Chapter 12. Regulation and Antitrust: The Role of Government in the Economy

60. In economics, an _____ is any good or commodity, transported from one country to another country in a legitimate fashion, typically for use in trade. _____ goods or services are provided to foreign consumers by domestic producers. _____ is an important part of international trade.
   a. ACEA agreement
   b. ACCRA Cost of Living Index
   c. AD-IA Model
   d. Export

61. The _____ is an economic and political union of 27 member states, located primarily in Europe. It was established by the Treaty of Maastricht on 1 November 1993, upon the foundations of the pre-existing European Economic Community. With a population of almost 500 million, the _____ generates an estimated 30% share (US$18.4 trillion in 2008) of the nominal gross world product.
   a. ACEA agreement
   b. European Union
   c. European Court of Justice
   d. ACCRA Cost of Living Index

62. _____ is exchange of capital, goods, and services across international borders or territories. In most countries, it represents a significant share of gross domestic product (GDP.) While _____ has been present throughout much of history, its economic, social, and political importance has been on the rise in recent centuries.
   a. Import license
   b. Intra-industry trade
   c. International Trade
   d. Incoterms

63. The _____ is an important selective, mainly private, international organization designed by its founders to supervise and liberalize international trade. The organization officially commenced on 1 January 1995, under the Marrakesh Agreement, succeeding the 1947 General Agreement on Tariffs and Trade (GATT.)

The _____ deals with regulation of trade between participating countries; it provides a framework for negotiating and formalising trade agreements, and a dispute resolution process aimed at enforcing participants' adherence to _____ agreements which are signed by representatives of member governments and ratified by their parliaments.

   a. Bio-energy village
   b. Backus-Kehoe-Kydland consumption correlation puzzle
   c. 2009 G-20 London summit protests
   d. World Trade Organization

64. The _____ is an international organization that oversees the global financial system by following the macroeconomic policies of its member countries, in particular those with an impact on exchange rates and the balance of payments. It is an organization formed to stabilize international exchange rates and facilitate development. It also offers financial and technical assistance to its members, making it an international lender of last resort.
   a. ACCRA Cost of Living Index
   b. ACEA agreement
   c. International Monetary Fund
   d. Office of Thrift Supervision

Chapter 13. Risk Analysis

1. _____ is a way of expressing knowledge or belief that an event will occur or has occurred. In mathematics the concept has been given an exact meaning in _____ theory, that is used extensively in such areas of study as mathematics, statistics, finance, gambling, science, and philosophy to draw conclusions about the likelihood of potential events and the underlying mechanics of complex systems.

The word _____ does not have a consistent direct definition.

   a. 130-30 fund
   b. 1921 recession
   c. 100-year flood
   d. Probability

2. In probability theory and statistics, a _____ identifies either the probability of each value of an unidentified random variable (when the variable is discrete), or the probability of the value falling within a particular interval (when the variable is continuous.) The _____ describes the range of possible values that a random variable can attain and the probability that the value of the random variable is within any (measurable) subset of that range. The Normal distribution, often called the 'bell curve'

When the random variable takes values in the set of real numbers, the _____ is completely described by the cumulative distribution function, whose value at each real x is the probability that the random variable is smaller than or equal to x.

   a. 1921 recession
   b. 130-30 fund
   c. 100-year flood
   d. Probability distribution

3. _____ refers to a company ceasing its operations following its inability to make a profit or to bring in enough revenue to cover its expenses.

Some businesses fail early on. This can occur as a result of poor management skills, insufficient marketing, inability to compete with other similar businesses, or a lack of interest from the public in the business's offerings.

   a. Golden Boot Compensation
   b. Small business
   c. Business process automation
   d. Business failure

4. In probability theory and statistics, _____ is a measure of the variability or dispersion of a population, a data set, or a probability distribution. A low _____ indicates that the data points tend to be very close to the same value (the mean), while high _____ indicates that the data are 'spread out' over a large range of values.

For example, the average height for adult men in the United States is about 70 inches, with a _____ of around 3 inches.

   a. 100-year flood
   b. Standard deviation
   c. 1921 recession
   d. 130-30 fund

5. which is known as the _____ distribution. When properly scaled and translated, the corresponding cumulative distribution function is known as the error function.

The Gaussian distribution is named for Carl Friedrich Gauss, who used it to analyze astronomical data, and defined the formula for its probability density function.

a. Standard normal
b. 130-30 fund
c. 1921 recession
d. 100-year flood

6. which is known as the _____. When properly scaled and translated, the corresponding cumulative distribution function is known as the error function.

The Gaussian distribution is named for Carl Friedrich Gauss, who used it to analyze astronomical data, and defined the formula for its probability density function.

a. 1921 recession
b. 100-year flood
c. Standard normal distribution
d. 130-30 fund

7. In probability theory and statistics, the _____ or Gaussian distribution is a continuous probability distribution that describes data that clusters around a mean or average. The graph of the associated probability density function is bell-shaped, with a peak at the mean, and is known as the Gaussian function or bell curve.

The _____ can be used to describe, at least approximately, any variable that tends to cluster around the mean.

a. 1921 recession
b. Normal distribution
c. 100-year flood
d. 130-30 fund

8. In mathematics, a _____ is a constant multiplicative factor of a certain object. For example, in the expression $9x^2$, the _____ of x^2 is 9.

The object can be such things as a variable, a vector, a function, etc.

a. 1921 recession
b. 130-30 fund
c. Coefficient
d. 100-year flood

9. The _____ variance model was first established in 1989, when Sir Dennis Weatherstone, the new chairman of J.P. Morgan, asked for a daily report measuring and explaining the risks of his firm. Nearly four years later in 1992, J.P. Morgan launched the _____ methodology to the marketplace, making the substantive research and analysis that satisfied Sir Dennis Weatherstone's request freely available to all market participants.

In 1998, as client demand for the group's risk management expertise exceeded the firm's internal risk management resources, _____ Group was spun off from J.P. Morgan.

a. Catastrophe modeling
b. Risk theory
c. Risk premium
d. RiskMetrics

Chapter 13. Risk Analysis

10. In economics, the _____ of a good or of a service is the utility of the specific use to which an agent would put a given increase in that good or service, or of the specific use that would be abandoned in response to a given decrease. In other words, _____ is the utility of the marginal use -- which, on the assumption of economic rationality, would be the least urgent use of the good or service, from the best feasible combination of actions in which its use is included. Under the mainstream assumptions, the _____ of a good or service is the posited quantified change in utility obtained by increasing or by decreasing use of that good or service.

    a. 100-year flood
    c. 1921 recession
    b. Marginal utility
    d. 130-30 fund

11. _____ is a concept in economics, finance, and psychology related to the behaviour of consumers and investors under uncertainty. _____ is the reluctance of a person to accept a bargain with an uncertain payoff rather than another bargain with a more certain, but possibly lower, expected payoff. For example, a risk-averse investor might choose to put his or her money into a bank account with a low but guaranteed interest rate, rather than into a stock that is likely to have high returns, but also has a chance of becoming worthless.

    a. Risk aversion
    c. Compound annual growth rate
    b. Reinsurance
    d. Risk theory

12. In economics, _____ behavior is in between risk aversion and risk seeking. If offered either â,¬50 or a 50% chance of â,¬100, a risk averse person will take the â,¬50, a risk seeking person will take the 50% chance of â,¬100, and a _____ person would have no preference between the two options.

In finance, when pricing an asset, a common technique is to figure out the probability of a future cash flow, then to discount that cash flow at the risk free rate.

    a. Risk neutral
    c. Transaction risk
    b. Currency risk
    d. Taleb distribution

13. In economics, _____ is a measure of the relative satisfaction from consumption of various goods and services. Given this measure, one may speak meaningfully of increasing or decreasing _____, and thereby explain economic behavior in terms of attempts to increase one's _____. For illustrative purposes, changes in _____ are sometimes expressed in units called utils.

    a. Ordinal utility
    c. Expected utility hypothesis
    b. Utility
    d. Utility function

14. In economics, game theory, and decision theory the _____ theorem or _____ hypothesis predicts that the 'betting preferences' of people with regard to uncertain outcomes (gambles) can be described by a mathematical relation which takes into account the size of a payout (whether in money or other goods), the probability of occurrence, risk aversion, and the different utility of the same payout to people with different assets or personal preferences. It is a more sophisticated theory than simply predicting that choices will be made based on expected value (which takes into account only the size of the payout and the probability of occurrence.)

Daniel Bernoulli described the complete theory in 1738.

    a. Expected utility hypothesis
    c. Ordinal utility
    b. Expected utility
    d. Utility

Chapter 13. Risk Analysis

15. _____, in law and economics, is a form of risk management primarily used to hedge against the risk of a contingent loss. _____ is defined as the equitable transfer of the risk of a loss, from one entity to another, in exchange for a premium, and can be thought of as a guaranteed small loss to prevent a large, possibly devastating loss. An insurer is a company selling the _____; an insured or policyholder is the person or entity buying the _____.
   - a. ACEA agreement
   - b. AD-IA Model
   - c. ACCRA Cost of Living Index
   - d. Insurance

16. _____ refers to a business or organization attempting to acquire goods or services to accomplish the goals of the enterprise. Though there are several organizations that attempt to set standards in the _____ process, processes can vary greatly between organizations. Typically the word '_____' is not used interchangeably with the word 'procurement', since procurement typically includes Expediting, Supplier Quality, and Traffic and Logistics (T'L) in addition to _____.
   - a. 130-30 fund
   - b. 100-year flood
   - c. Free port
   - d. Purchasing

17. A _____ is the minimum difference a person requires to be willing to take an uncertain bet, between the expected value of the bet and the certain value that he is indifferent to.

The certainty equivalent is the guaranteed payoff at which a person is 'indifferent' between accepting the guaranteed payoff and a higher but uncertain payoff. (It is the amount of the higher payout minus the _____.)

   - a. Risk premium
   - b. Linear model
   - c. Ruin theory
   - d. Workers compensation

18. Discounting is a financial mechanism in which a debtor obtains the right to delay payments to a creditor, for a defined period of time, in exchange for a charge or fee. Essentially, the party that owes money in the present purchases the right to delay the payment until some future date. The _____, or charge, is simply the difference between the original amount owed in the present and the amount that has to be paid in the future to settle the debt.
   - a. Reliability theory
   - b. Reinsurance
   - c. Certified Risk Manager
   - d. Discount

19. The _____ is an interest rate a central bank charges depository institutions that borrow reserves from it.

The term _____ has two meanings:

- the same as interest rate; the term 'discount' does not refer to the meaning of the word, but to the purpose of using the quantity, such as computations of present value, e.g. net present value or discounted cash flow

- the annual effective _____, which is the annual interest divided by the capital including that interest; this rate is lower than the interest rate; it corresponds to using the value after a year as the nominal value, and seeing the initial value as the nominal value minus a discount; it is used for Treasury Bills and similar financial instruments

The annual effective _____ is the annual interest divided by the capital including that interest, which is the interest rate divided by 100% plus the interest rate. It is the annual discount factor to be applied to the future cash flow, to find the discount, subtracted from a future value to find the value one year earlier.

For example, suppose there is a government bond that sells for $95 and pays $100 in a year's time.

a. Stochastic volatility
b. Johansen test
c. Perpetuity
d. Discount rate

20. A _____ is a situation that involves losing one quality or aspect of something in return for gaining another quality or aspect. It implies a decision to be made with full comprehension of both the upside and downside of a particular choice.

In economics the term is expressed as opportunity cost, referring the most preferred alternative given up.

a. Friedman-Savage utility function
b. Nonmarket
c. Whitemail
d. Trade-off

21. _____ is the probability of some event A, given the occurrence of some other event B. _____ is written P(A|B), and is read 'the probability of A, given B'.

Joint probability is the probability of two events in conjunction. That is, it is the probability of both events together.

a. Memorylessness
b. Density function
c. Marginal likelihood
d. Conditional probability

22. In statistics, _____ refers to techniques for the modeling and analysis of numerical data consisting of values of a dependent variable and of one or more independent variables The dependent variable in the regression equation is modeled as a function of the independent variables, corresponding parameters, and an error term. The error term is treated as a random variable.

a. 100-year flood
b. 130-30 fund
c. 1921 recession
d. Regression analysis

23. _____ is a decision rule used in decision theory, game theory, statistics and philosophy for minimizing the maximum possible loss. Alternatively, it can be thought of as maximizing the minimum gain (maximin.) It started from two-player zero-sum game theory, covering both the cases where players take alternate moves and those where they make simultaneous moves.

a. 100-year flood
b. 130-30 fund
c. Design Impact Measures
d. Minimax

24. In microeconomics, _____ is quite simply the conversion of inputs into outputs. It is an economic process that uses resources to create a good or service that is suitable for exchange. This can include manufacturing, storing, shipping, and packaging.

a. Red Guards
b. Production
c. Solved
d. MET

Chapter 13. Risk Analysis

25. In economics, a _____ is a function that specifies the output of a firm, an industry, or an entire economy for all combinations of inputs. A meta-_____ compares the practice of the existing entities converting inputs X into output y to determine the most efficient practice _____ of the existing entities, whether the most efficient feasible practice production or the most efficient actual practice production. In either case, the maximum output of a technologically-determined production process is a mathematical function of input factors of production.
   a. Constant elasticity of substitution
   b. Short-run
   c. Post-Fordism
   d. Production function

26. A security is a fungible, negotiable instrument representing financial value. _____ are broadly categorized into debt _____; equity _____, e.g., common stocks; and derivative (finance) contracts such as forwards, futures, options and swaps. The company or other entity issuing the security is called the issuer.
   a. Settlement risk
   b. Securities
   c. Red herring prospectus
   d. Pass-Through Certificates

27. The U.S. _____ is an independent agency of the United States government which holds primary responsibility for enforcing the federal securities laws and regulating the securities industry, the nation's stock and options exchanges, and other electronic securities markets. The SEC was created by section 4 of the Securities Exchange Act of 1934 (now codified as 15 U.S.C. § 78d and commonly referred to as the 1934 Act.)
   a. Securities and Exchange Commission
   b. 100-year flood
   c. 1921 recession
   d. 130-30 fund

28. _____ is an online peer-reviewed magazine published by the Agricultural ' Applied Economics Association (AAEA) for readers interested in the policy and management of agriculture, the food industry, natural resources, rural communities, and the environment. _____ is published quarterly and is available free online. It is currently one of three outreach products offered by AAEA, along with the more timely Policy Issues and the forthcoming Shared Materials section of the AAEA Web site.
   a. 100-year flood
   b. 1921 recession
   c. Choices
   d. 130-30 fund

29. To _____ is to impose a financial charge or other levy upon a taxpayer by a state or the functional equivalent of a state.

_____es are also imposed by many subnational entities. _____es consist of direct _____ or indirect _____, and may be paid in money or as its labour equivalent (often but not always unpaid.)

   a. 130-30 fund
   b. Tax
   c. 1921 recession
   d. 100-year flood

30. _____ is sometimes referred to as _____, actually it means Economic Monetary Union.

First ideas of an economic and monetary union in Europe were raised well before establishing the European Communities. For example, already in the League of Nations, Gustav Stresemann asked in 1929 for a European currency (Link) against the background of an increased economic division due to a number of new nation states in Europe after WWI.

a. European Monetary System
b. Euro Interbank Offered Rate
c. Exchange rate mechanism
d. European Monetary Union

31. A _____ is an agreement between two parties to buy or sell an asset at a specified point of time in the future. The price of the underlying instrument, in whatever form, is paid before control of the instrument changes. This is one of the many forms of buy/sell orders where the time of trade is not the time where the securities themselves are exchanged.
a. Delta One
b. Risk-neutral measure
c. Notional amount
d. Forward contract

32. An economic and _____ is a single market with a common currency. It is to be distinguished from a mere currency union, which does not involve a single market. This is the fifth stage of economic integration.
a. Customs union
b. Monetary Union
c. Commercial invoice
d. Free trade zone

33. In finance, a _____ is a standardized contract, to buy or sell a specified commodity of standardized quality at a certain date in the future, at a market determined price (the futures price.)

The price is determined by the instantaneous equilibrium between the forces of supply and demand among competing buy and sell orders on the exchange at the time of the purchase or sale of the contract.

In many cases, the items may be such non-traditional 'commodities' as foreign currencies, commercial or government paper [e.g., bonds], or 'baskets' of corporate equity ['stock indices'] or other financial instruments.

a. Local volatility
b. Dual currency deposit
c. Power reverse dual currency note
d. Futures contract

34. _____ was a U.S. hedge fund which used trading strategies such as fixed income arbitrage, statistical arbitrage, and pairs trading, combined with high leverage. It failed spectacularly in the late 1990s, leading to a massive bailout by other major banks and investment houses, which was supervised by the Federal Reserve.

LTCM was founded in 1994 by John Meriwether, the former vice-chairman and head of bond trading at Salomon Brothers.

a. General purpose technologies
b. Collectivization of agriculture in Romania
c. Consumer protection
d. Long-Term Capital Management

35. _____ describes a deliberate attempt to interfere with the free and fair operation of the market and create artificial, false or misleading appearances with respect to the price of a security, commodity or currency. _____ is prohibited under Section 9(a)(2) of the Securities Exchange Act of 1934, and in Australia under Section s 1041A of the Corporations Act 2001. The Act defines _____ as transactions which create an artificial price or maintain an artificial price for a tradable security.
a. Managerial economics
b. Legal monopoly
c. Net domestic product
d. Market manipulation

Chapter 13. Risk Analysis

36. 'The _____: Quality Uncertainty and the Market Mechanism' is a 1970 paper by the economist George Akerlof. It discusses information asymmetry, which occurs when the seller knows more about a product than the buyer. Akerlof, Michael Spence, and Joseph Stiglitz jointly received the Nobel Memorial Prize in Economic Sciences in 2001 for their research related to asymmetric information.
    a. 100-year flood
    b. 130-30 fund
    c. 1921 recession
    d. Market for lemons

37. _____, anti-selection insurance, statistics, and risk management. It refers to a market process in which 'bad' results occur when buyers and sellers have asymmetric information (i.e. access to different information): the 'bad' products or customers are more likely to be selected. A bank that sets one price for all its checking account customers runs the risk of being adversely selected against by its low-balance, high-activity (and hence least profitable) customers.
    a. Adverse selection
    b. AD-IA Model
    c. ACCRA Cost of Living Index
    d. ACEA agreement

38. _____ is the prospect that a party insulated from risk may behave differently from the way it would behave if it were fully exposed to the risk. In insurance, _____ that occurs without conscious or malicious action is called morale hazard.

    _____ is related to information asymmetry, a situation in which one party in a transaction has more information than another.

    a. 130-30 fund
    b. 100-year flood
    c. 1921 recession
    d. Moral hazard

39. The _____ (often called 'the Chicago Merc,' or 'the Merc') is an American financial and commodity derivative exchange based in Chicago. The _____ was founded in 1898 as the Chicago Butter and Egg Board. Originally, the exchange was a non-profit organization.
    a. Chicago Mercantile Exchange
    b. South Sea Company
    c. New Economic Policy
    d. Delancey Street Foundation

40. A _____ is something for which there is demand, but which is supplied without qualitative differentiation across a market. It is a product that is the same no matter who produces it, such as petroleum, notebook paper, or milk. In other words, copper is copper.
    a. Commodity
    b. 100-year flood
    c. Hard commodity
    d. Soft commodity

41. The _____ consists of a number of economic theories which describe the nature of the firm, company including its existence, its behaviour, and its relationship with the market.

    In simplified terms, the _____ aims to answer these questions:

    1. Existence - why do firms emerge, why are not all transactions in the economy mediated over the market?
    2. Boundaries - why the boundary between firms and the market is located exactly there? Which transactions are performed internally and which are negotiated on the market?
    3. Organization - why are firms structured in such specific way? What is the interplay of formal and informal relationships?

Despite looking simple, these questions are not answered by the established economic theory, which usually views firms as given, and treats them as black boxes without any internal structure.

The First World War period saw a change of emphasis in economic theory away from industry-level analysis which mainly included analysing markets to analysis at the level of the firm, as it became increasingly clear that perfect competition was no longer an adequate model of how firms behaved. Economic theory till then had focussed on trying to understand markets alone and there had been little study on understanding why firms or organisations exist.

- a. Technology gap
- b. Khazzoom-Brookes postulate
- c. Theory of the firm
- d. Policy Ineffectiveness Proposition

42. A _____ is an investment fund open to a limited range of investors that is permitted by regulators to undertake a wider range of investment and trading activities than other investment funds and pays a performance fee to its investment manager. Each fund has its own strategy which determines the type of investments and the methods of investment it undertakes. _____s, as a class, invest in a broad range of investments including shares, debt, commodities and so forth.
- a. 100-year flood
- b. Hedge Fund
- c. 130-30 fund
- d. 1921 recession

43. _____, in economics, is the period of time required for economic agents to reallocate resources, and generally reestablish equilibrium.

The actual length of this period, usually numbered in years or decades, varies widely depending on circumstantial context. During the _____, all factors are variable.

- a. Government surplus
- b. Producer surplus
- c. Temporary equilibrium method
- d. Long Term

Chapter 14. Long-Run Investment Decisions: Capital Budgeting

1. _____ is the planning process used to determine whether a firm's long term investments such as new machinery, replacement machinery, new plants, new products, and research development projects are worth pursuing. It is budget for major capital, or investment, expenditures.

Many formal methods are used in _____, including the techniques such as

- Net present value
- Profitability index
- Internal rate of return
- Modified Internal Rate of Return
- Equivalent annuity

These methods use the incremental cash flows from each potential investment, or project. Techniques based on accounting earnings and accounting rules are sometimes used - though economists consider this to be improper - such as the accounting rate of return, and 'return on investment.' Simplified and hybrid methods are used as well, such as payback period and discounted payback period.

a. Preferred stock
b. Voting interest
c. Capital budgeting
d. Participating preferred stock

2. In economics and finance, _____ is the change in total cost that arises when the quantity produced changes by one unit. It is the cost of producing one more unit of a good. Mathematically, the _____ function is expressed as the first derivative of the total cost (TC) function with respect to quantity (Q.)

a. Khozraschyot
b. Variable cost
c. Quality costs
d. Marginal cost

3. The _____ is an expected return that the provider of capital plans to earn on their investment.

Capital (money) used for funding a business should earn returns for the capital providers who risk their capital. For an investment to be worthwhile, the expected return on capital must be greater than the _____.

a. Modigliani-Miller theorem
b. Capital expenditure
c. Capital intensive
d. Cost of capital

4. _____ refers to the movement of cash into or out of a business or financial product. It is usually measured during a specified, finite period of time. Measurement of _____ can be used

- to determine a project's rate of return or value. The time of _____s into and out of projects are used as inputs in financial models such as internal rate of return, and net present value.
- to determine problems with a business's liquidity. Being profitable does not necessarily mean being liquid. A company can fail because of a shortage of cash, even while profitable.
- as an alternate measure of a business's profits when it is believed that accrual accounting concepts do not represent economic realities. For example, a company may be notionally profitable but generating little operational cash (as may be the case for a company that barters its products rather than selling for cash.) In such a case, the company may be deriving additional operating cash by issuing shares evaluating default risk, re-investment requirements, etc.

_____ is a generic term used differently depending on the context. It may be defined by users for their own purposes.

a. Cash flow
c. Second lien loan
b. Strip financing
d. Restricted stock

5. _____ is a term that refers both to:

- a formal discipline used to help appraise, or assess, the case for a project or proposal, which itself is a process known as project appraisal; and
- an informal approach to making decisions of any kind.

Under both definitions the process involves, whether explicitly or implicitly, weighing the total expected costs against the total expected benefits of one or more actions in order to choose the best or most profitable option. The formal process is often referred to as either CBA (_____) or BCost-benefit analysis

A hallmark of CBA is that all benefits and all costs are expressed in money terms, and are adjusted for the time value of money, so that all flows of benefits and flows of project costs over time (which tend to occur at different points in time) are expressed on a common basis in terms of their e;present value.e; Closely related, but slightly different, formal techniques include Cost-effectiveness analysis, Economic impact analysis, Fiscal impact analysis and Social Return on Investment(SROI) analysis. The latter builds upon the logic of _____, but differs in that it is explicitly designed to inform the practical decision-making of enterprise managers and investors focused on optimising their social and environmental impacts.

a. Decision theory
c. 130-30 fund
b. 100-year flood
d. Cost-benefit analysis

6. The _____ is an agency of the United States government, responsible for the nation's public space program. NASA was established on July 29, 1958, by the National Aeronautics and Space Act.

In addition to the space program, it is also responsible for long-term civilian and military aerospace research.

a. H.R. 5405
c. Commodity trading advisors
b. National Aeronautics and Space Administration
d. Consumption

7. _____ or net present worth (NPW) is defined as the total present value (PV) of a time series of cash flows. It is a standard method for using the time value of money to appraise long-term projects. Used for capital budgeting, and widely throughout economics, it measures the excess or shortfall of cash flows, in present value terms, once financing charges are met.

a. Maturity
c. Future value
b. Refinancing risk
d. Net present value

Chapter 14. Long-Run Investment Decisions: Capital Budgeting

8. Simply put, _____ is the value of money figuring in a given amount of interest for a given amount of time. For example 100 dollars of todays money held for a year at 5 percent interest is worth 105 dollars, therefore 100 dollars paid now or 105 dollars paid exactly one year from now is the same amount of payment of money with that given intersest at that given amount of time. This notion dates at least to Martín de Azpilcueta of the School of Salamanca.

a. Time value of money
b. 100-year flood
c. Newtonian time
d. Time Banking

9. _____ is the value on a given date of a future payment or series of future payments, discounted to reflect the time value of money and other factors such as investment risk. _____ calculations are widely used in business and economics to provide a means to compare cash flows at different times on a meaningful 'like to like' basis.

Money value fluctuates over time: $100 today are not worth $100 in five years.

a. Present value
b. Present value of costs
c. Tax shield
d. Future value

10. _____ is the a method of technical and economic research of the systems for purpose to optimize a parity between system's consumer functions or properties and expenses to achieve those functions or properties.

This methodology for continuous perfection of production, industrial technologies, organizational structures was developed by Juryj Sobolev in 1948 at the 'Perm telephone factory'

- 1948 Juryj Sobolev - the first success in application of a method analysis at the 'Perm telephone factory' .
- 1949 - the first application for the invention as result of use of the new method.

Today in economically developed countries practically each enterprise or the company use methodology of the kind of functional-cost analysis as a practice of the quality management, most full satisfying to principles of standards of series ISO 9000.

- Interest of consumer not in products itself, but the advantage which it will receive from its usage.
- The consumer aspires to reduce his expenses
- Functions needed by consumer can be executed in the various ways, and, hence, with various efficiency and expenses. Among possible alternatives of realization of functions exist such in which the parity of quality and the price is the optimal for the consumer.

The goal of _____ is achievement of the highest consumer satisfaction of production at simultaneous decrease in all kinds of industrial expenses Classical _____ has three English synonyms - Value Engineering, Value Management, Value Analysis.

a. Staple financing
b. Monopoly wage
c. Willingness to pay
d. Function cost analysis

11. In finance, _____ rate of profit or sometimes just return, is the ratio of money gained or lost on an investment relative to the amount of money invested. The amount of money gained or lost may be referred to as interest, profit/loss, gain/loss, or net income/loss. The money invested may be referred to as the asset, capital, principal, or the cost basis of the investment.
   a. Cost accrual ratio
   b. Current ratio
   c. Sortino ratio
   d. Rate of return

12. The _____ consists of a number of economic theories which describe the nature of the firm, company including its existence, its behaviour, and its relationship with the market.

In simplified terms, the _____ aims to answer these questions:

1. Existence - why do firms emerge, why are not all transactions in the economy mediated over the market?
2. Boundaries - why the boundary between firms and the market is located exactly there? Which transactions are performed internally and which are negotiated on the market?
3. Organization - why are firms structured in such specific way? What is the interplay of formal and informal relationships?

Despite looking simple, these questions are not answered by the established economic theory, which usually views firms as given, and treats them as black boxes without any internal structure.

The First World War period saw a change of emphasis in economic theory away from industry-level analysis which mainly included analysing markets to analysis at the level of the firm, as it became increasingly clear that perfect competition was no longer an adequate model of how firms behaved. Economic theory till then had focussed on trying to understand markets alone and there had been little study on understanding why firms or organisations exist.

   a. Policy Ineffectiveness Proposition
   b. Technology gap
   c. Khazzoom-Brookes postulate
   d. Theory of the firm

13. _____ refers to the stock of skills and knowledge embodied in the ability to perform labor so as to produce economic value. It is the skills and knowledge gained by a worker through education and experience. Many early economic theories refer to it simply as labor, one of three factors of production, and consider it to be a fungible resource -- homogeneous and easily interchangeable. Other conceptions of labor dispense with these assumptions.
   a. Law of increasing costs
   b. Human capital
   c. Price theory
   d. General equilibrium

14. _____ identifies the relationship of investment to payoff of a proposed project. The ratio is calculated as follows:

$$\text{Profitability index} = \frac{\text{PV of future cash flows}}{\text{PV of initial investment}}$$

Chapter 14. Long-Run Investment Decisions: Capital Budgeting 101

_____ is also known as Profit Investment Ratio, abbreviated to P.I. and Value Investment Ratio (V.I.R.). _____ is a good tool for ranking projects because it allows you to clearly identify the amount of value created per unit of investment, thus if you are capital constrained you wish to invest in those projects which create value most efficiently first.

Nota Bene; Statements below this paragraph assume the cash flow calculated does not include the investment made in the project.

a. Market if touched
c. Financial Reporting

b. Multi-Currency Pricing
d. Profitability index

15. _____ is the controlled distribution of resources and scarce goods or services. _____ controls the size of the ration, one's allotted portion of the resources being distributed on a particular day or at a particular time.

In economics, it is often common to use the word '_____' to refer to one of the roles that prices play in markets, while _____ is called 'non-price _____.' Using prices to ration means that those with the most money (or other assets) and who want a product the most are first to receive it.

a. Rationing
c. 1921 recession

b. 100-year flood
d. 130-30 fund

16. _____ is that which is owed; usually referencing assets owed, but the term can also cover moral obligations and other interactions not requiring money. In the case of assets, _____ is a means of using future purchasing power in the present before a summation has been earned. Some companies and corporations use _____ as a part of their overall corporate finance strategy.

a. Hard money loan
c. Collateral Management

b. Debenture
d. Debt

17. In finance, the _____ is the minimum rate of return a firm must offer shareholders to compensate for waiting for their returns, and for bearing some risk.

The _____ capital for a particular company is the rate of return on investment that is required by the company's ordinary shareholders. The return consists both of dividend and capital gains, e.g. increases in the share price.

a. Gross operating surplus
c. Derived demand

b. Seasonal industry
d. Cost of equity

18. _____ is the concept or idea of fairness in economics, particularly as to taxation or welfare economics.

In welfare economics, _____ may be distinguished from economic efficiency in overall evaluation of social welfare. Although '_____' has broader uses, it may be posed as a counterpart to economic inequality in yielding a 'good' distribution of welfare.

Chapter 14. Long-Run Investment Decisions: Capital Budgeting

a. ACEA agreement
c. AD-IA Model
b. ACCRA Cost of Living Index
d. Equity

19. _____s are payments made by a corporation to its shareholders. It is the portion of corporate profits paid out to stockholders. When a corporation earns a profit or surplus, that money can be put to two uses: it can either be re-invested in the business (called retained earnings), or it can be paid to the shareholders as a _____.
   a. Dividend cover
   b. Dividend
   c. Dividend yield
   d. Dividend puzzle

20. The term _____ has three unrelated technical definitions, and is also used in a variety of non-technical ways.

   - In financial economics, it refers to any asset used to make money, as opposed to assets used for personal enjoyment or consumption. This is an important distinction because two people can disagree sharply about the value of personal assets, one person might think a sports car is more valuable than a pickup truck, another person might have the opposite taste. But if an asset is held for the purpose of making money, taste has nothing to do with it, only differences of opinion about how much money the asset will produce. With the further assumption that people agree on the probability distribution of future cash flows, it is possible to have an objective _____ pricing model. Even without the assumption of agreement, it is possible to set rational limits on _____ value.
   - In governmental accounting, it is defined as any asset used in operations with an initial useful life extending beyond one reporting period. Generally, government managers have a 'stewardship' duty to maintain _____s under their control. See International Public Sector Accounting Standards for details.
   - In US tax accounting, it is defined as any property other than a list of exceptions. The main exceptions are anything held for sale, and any real estate or depreciable property used in business. Almost everything you own and use for personal purposes, pleasure or investment is a _____. If something is a _____ for tax purposes, gains or losses on sale or disposition are capital gains or capital losses. For individuals, however, capital losses on property held for personal use are generally not deductible. See the IRS publication Tax Facts about Capital Gains and Losses for details.

A well-known financial accounting textbook advises that the term be avoided except in tax accounting because it is used in so many different senses, not all of them well-defined. For example it is often used as a synonym for fixed assets or for investments in securities.

A common non-technical usage occurs when people ask that employees or the environment or something else be treated as a _____.

   a. Consumption beta
   b. Capital asset
   c. Dynamic asset allocation
   d. Mid price

21. In finance, the _____ is used to determine a theoretically appropriate required rate of return of an asset, if that asset is to be added to an already well-diversified portfolio, given that asset's non-diversifiable risk. The model takes into account the asset's sensitivity to non-diversifiable risk (also known as systemic risk or market risk), often represented by the quantity beta (β) in the financial industry, as well as the expected return of the market and the expected return of a theoretical risk-free asset.

Chapter 14. Long-Run Investment Decisions: Capital Budgeting

The model was introduced by Jack Treynor (1961, 1962), William Sharpe (1964), John Lintner (1965a,b) and Jan Mossin (1966) independently, building on the earlier work of Harry Markowitz on diversification and modern portfolio theory.

a. Martingale pricing
c. Ho-Lee model

b. Capital asset pricing model
d. Fama-MacBeth regression

22. In microeconomics, _____ is quite simply the conversion of inputs into outputs. It is an economic process that uses resources to create a good or service that is suitable for exchange. This can include manufacturing, storing, shipping, and packaging.

a. MET
c. Solved

b. Red Guards
d. Production

23. In economics, a _____ is a function that specifies the output of a firm, an industry, or an entire economy for all combinations of inputs. A meta-_____ compares the practice of the existing entities converting inputs X into output y to determine the most efficient practice _____ of the existing entities, whether the most efficient feasible practice production or the most efficient actual practice production. In either case, the maximum output of a technologically-determined production process is a mathematical function of input factors of production.

a. Short-run
c. Post-Fordism

b. Constant elasticity of substitution
d. Production function

24. In business and accounting, _____ are everything of value that is owned by a person or company. It is a claim on the property your income of a borrower. The balance sheet of a firm records the monetary value of the _____ owned by the firm.

a. ACCRA Cost of Living Index
c. Amortization schedule

b. ACEA agreement
d. Assets

25. In mathematics, a _____ is a constant multiplicative factor of a certain object. For example, in the expression $9x^2$, the _____ of x^2 is 9.

The object can be such things as a variable, a vector, a function, etc.

a. 1921 recession
c. 100-year flood

b. 130-30 fund
d. Coefficient

26. _____ is one of the four Ps of the marketing mix. The other three aspects are product, promotion, and place. It is also a key variable in microeconomic price allocation theory.

a. Premium pricing
c. Pricing

b. Point of total assumption
d. Guaranteed Maximum Price

27. _____ is the average weighted of cost of equity capital (ke) and cost of debt (kd.)

According to the 'Modigliani-Miller theorem', under certain assumptions a firm's WACC remains constant regardless of changes in its capital structure. These assumptions are outlined below:

1. Assume no individual or corporate taxes
2. Assume that individuals are able to borrow at the same rate as the firm, (known as home-made gearing)
3. Assume that the market is frictionless, that is no there are no transaction costs
4. Assume that the company has a fixed investment policy being implemented in the strategy of the company

Furthermore, M'M theory hypotheses that the cost of equity capital does change as the company increase its gearing level in the same direction of the gearing level. The reason is that as a company increases its leverage, the shareholders require a higher rate of return because the higher fixed interest costs lead to a higher variance in earnings.

a. Method of simulated moments
b. Seemingly unrelated regression
c. Censored regression models
d. Weighted cost of capital

28. In game theory, _____ is a solution concept of a game involving two or more players, in which each player is assumed to know the equilibrium strategies of the other players, and no player has anything to gain by changing only his or her own strategy unilaterally. If each player has chosen a strategy and no player can benefit by changing his or her strategy while the other players keep theirs unchanged, then the current set of strategy choices and the corresponding payoffs constitute a _____.

Stated simply, Amy and Bill are in _____ if Amy is making the best decision she can, taking into account Bill's decision, and Bill is making the best decision he can, taking into account Amy's decision.

a. Linear production game
b. Proper equilibrium
c. Lump of labour
d. Nash equilibrium

29. _____ is an online peer-reviewed magazine published by the Agricultural ' Applied Economics Association (AAEA) for readers interested in the policy and management of agriculture, the food industry, natural resources, rural communities, and the environment. _____ is published quarterly and is available free online. It is currently one of three outreach products offered by AAEA, along with the more timely Policy Issues and the forthcoming Shared Materials section of the AAEA Web site.

a. 100-year flood
b. Choices
c. 1921 recession
d. 130-30 fund

30. _____ is a comparative concept of the ability and performance of a firm, sub-sector or country to sell and supply goods and/or services in a given market. Although widely used in economics and business management, the usefulness of the concept, particularly in the context of national _____, is vigorously disputed by economists, such as Paul Krugman .

The term may also be applied to markets, where it is used to refer to the extent to which the market structure may be regarded as perfectly competitive.

Chapter 14. Long-Run Investment Decisions: Capital Budgeting

a. Competitiveness
c. Quota share
b. Debt moratorium
d. Countervailing duties

31.

The net present value (NPV) of all of a company's customers in terms of customer loyalty and indirectly, the revenue that the company can obtain from them. _____ is the total of the discounted lifetime values of all of the firm's customers.

In deciding the value of a company, it is important to know of how much value its customer base is in terms of future revenues.

a. Product proliferation
c. Marginal revenue
b. Customer equity
d. Temporary equilibrium method

32. The _____ is an economic and political union of 27 member states, located primarily in Europe. It was established by the Treaty of Maastricht on 1 November 1993, upon the foundations of the pre-existing European Economic Community. With a population of almost 500 million, the _____ generates an estimated 30% share (US$18.4 trillion in 2008) of the nominal gross world product.

a. European Union
c. European Court of Justice
b. ACEA agreement
d. ACCRA Cost of Living Index

33. _____ is a branch of economics with three main subdisciplines international trade, monetary economics and international finance.

- International trade studies goods-and-services flows across international boundaries from supply-and-demand factors, economic integration, and policy variables such as tariff rates and trade quotas.
- International finance studies the flow of capital across international financial markets, and the effects of these movements on exchange rates.
- International monetary economics and macroeconomics studies money and macro flows across countries.
- Stanley W. Black (2008.) 'international monetary institutions,' The New Palgrave Dictionary of Economics. 2nd Edition.

a. Index number
c. ACCRA Cost of Living Index
b. International economics
d. Economic depreciation

34. _____s is the social science that studies the production, distribution, and consumption of goods and services. The term _____s comes from the Ancient Greek oá¼°κονομῖα from oá¼¶κος (oikos, 'house') + vĺŒμος (nomos, 'custom' or 'law'), hence 'rules of the house(hold)'. Current _____ models developed out of the broader field of political economy in the late 19th century, owing to a desire to use an empirical approach more akin to the physical sciences.

a. Opportunity cost
c. Inflation
b. Energy economics
d. Economic

35. The term _____ refers to an offense under Section 2 of the American Sherman Antitrust Act, passed in 1890. Section 2 states that any person 'who shall monopolize .

a. Bilateral monopoly
c. Quasi-rent

b. Complementary monopoly
d. Monopolization

ANSWER KEY

Chapter 1

1. a	2. d	3. d	4. a	5. c	6. a	7. c	8. d	9. c	10. b
11. d	12. b	13. d	14. d	15. d	16. d	17. d	18. a	19. a	20. d
21. a	22. a	23. a	24. d	25. d	26. d	27. c	28. a	29. d	30. b
31. b	32. d	33. d	34. d	35. c	36. b	37. d	38. d	39. a	40. a
41. d	42. b	43. d	44. d	45. d					

Chapter 2

1. d	2. d	3. d	4. d	5. b	6. a	7. d	8. a	9. a	10. d
11. a	12. d	13. a	14. b	15. a	16. d	17. d	18. d	19. d	20. d
21. b	22. c	23. d	24. d	25. b	26. d	27. c	28. c	29. c	

Chapter 3

1. a	2. d	3. d	4. d	5. d	6. d	7. b	8. b	9. d	10. c
11. a	12. a	13. b	14. d	15. c	16. c	17. a	18. d	19. d	20. c
21. d	22. d	23. c	24. d	25. a	26. d	27. d	28. d	29. d	30. d

Chapter 4

1. b	2. d	3. c	4. a	5. d	6. d	7. b	8. b	9. b	10. d
11. c	12. a	13. d	14. c	15. d	16. d	17. d	18. d	19. d	20. a
21. b	22. d	23. d	24. d	25. d	26. c	27. b			

Chapter 5

1. a	2. b	3. d	4. d	5. d	6. d	7. d	8. c	9. d	10. d
11. d	12. d	13. d	14. b	15. d	16. c	17. d	18. d	19. d	20. d
21. d	22. a	23. d	24. c	25. d	26. a	27. b	28. c		

Chapter 6

1. d	2. d	3. a	4. a	5. a	6. b	7. c	8. a	9. d	10. d
11. a	12. d	13. d	14. b	15. a	16. a	17. b	18. a	19. b	20. a
21. d	22. c	23. b	24. c	25. d	26. b	27. d	28. a	29. d	30. a
31. c									

Chapter 7

1. b	2. b	3. a	4. d	5. d	6. d	7. d	8. a	9. b	10. d
11. d	12. d	13. d	14. d	15. b	16. a	17. c	18. d	19. a	20. d
21. a	22. a	23. a	24. b	25. d	26. d	27. c	28. a	29. d	30. d
31. d	32. a	33. a	34. b	35. d					

Chapter 8

1. d	2. d	3. c	4. d	5. d	6. b	7. d	8. b	9. a	10. d
11. a	12. c	13. c	14. c	15. d	16. b	17. d	18. a	19. d	20. d
21. a	22. b	23. d	24. a	25. b	26. c	27. d	28. c	29. d	30. c
31. c	32. b	33. d	34. c						

Chapter 9

1. d	2. b	3. c	4. d	5. a	6. b	7. d	8. b	9. a	10. a
11. c	12. d	13. b	14. d	15. d	16. a	17. d	18. d	19. b	20. b
21. d	22. a	23. c	24. a	25. d	26. d	27. b	28. a	29. c	30. b
31. d	32. c	33. a	34. d	35. d	36. d				

Chapter 10

1. c	2. d	3. d	4. d	5. d	6. d	7. b	8. d	9. d	10. a
11. a	12. b	13. a	14. d	15. b					

Chapter 11

1. b	2. c	3. c	4. d	5. c	6. a	7. d	8. a	9. d	10. a
11. c	12. d	13. d	14. d	15. a	16. d	17. c	18. c	19. b	20. d
21. c	22. d	23. a	24. b	25. d	26. a	27. d			

Chapter 12

1. b	2. d	3. a	4. d	5. a	6. d	7. a	8. d	9. b	10. c
11. d	12. c	13. b	14. d	15. c	16. d	17. d	18. c	19. d	20. c
21. d	22. d	23. b	24. b	25. b	26. d	27. b	28. d	29. d	30. b
31. a	32. d	33. d	34. d	35. d	36. d	37. b	38. c	39. a	40. d
41. d	42. d	43. a	44. a	45. b	46. b	47. d	48. d	49. c	50. d
51. c	52. d	53. b	54. a	55. d	56. d	57. d	58. c	59. a	60. d
61. b	62. c	63. d	64. c						

Chapter 13

1. d	2. d	3. d	4. b	5. a	6. c	7. b	8. c	9. d	10. b
11. a	12. a	13. b	14. b	15. d	16. d	17. a	18. d	19. d	20. d
21. d	22. d	23. d	24. b	25. d	26. b	27. a	28. c	29. b	30. d
31. d	32. b	33. d	34. d	35. d	36. d	37. a	38. d	39. a	40. a
41. c	42. b	43. d							

Chapter 14

1. c	2. d	3. d	4. a	5. d	6. b	7. d	8. a	9. a	10. d
11. d	12. d	13. b	14. d	15. a	16. d	17. d	18. d	19. b	20. b
21. b	22. d	23. d	24. d	25. d	26. c	27. d	28. d	29. b	30. a
31. b	32. a	33. b	34. d	35. d					

www.ingramcontent.com/pod-product-compliance
Lightning Source LLC
Chambersburg PA
CBHW081204240426
43669CB00039B/2812